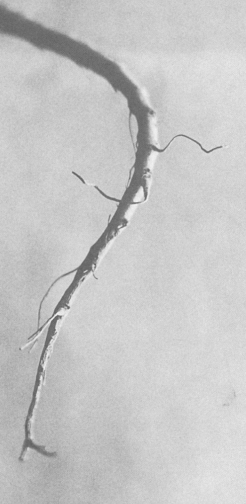

THE
SPROUTED
KITCHEN

THE
SPROUTED
KITCHEN

a tastier take  on whole foods

sara forte

photography by
hugh forte

TEN SPEED PRESS
Berkeley

Dedicated to my beloved, Hugh,
my constant encouragement, talented photographer,
and ceaseless eater.

For without you inspiring me to go after
what I love, I would still be sitting in a windowless
cubicle from 8 to 5, far away from these pages.
I love you.

"I still think that one of the pleasantest of all emotions is to know that I, I with my brain and my hands, have nourished my beloved few, that I have concocted a stew or a story, a rarity or a plain dish, to sustain them truly against the hungers of the world."
—M. K. FISHER

contents

a bit about the sprouted kitchen

If you knew my family's culinary history, you would think that the idea of me writing a cookbook is a bit ironic. My dad prefers spaghetti sauce from one of those powder packets, and my mom prepared a lot of frozen taquitos throughout my childhood. We always sat down to meals as a family, and it's not that we didn't eat well, but I don't have an heirloom box of family recipes, if you catch my drift.

I became passionate about both the creative process of cooking and the nutritional aspects of food once I left for college and started cooking for myself. I began working at the organic farm on campus, and I taught myself how to use the incredible seasonal produce we grew, much of which was new to me. This was right around the time when Community Supported Agriculture (CSA) boxes began cropping up in most people's field of view, and the community of people who cared deeply about their food was expanding quickly. (I'm still pretty young, so I'm not going to say I was on the cutting edge of the food movement by any means, but we can all agree that an interest in healthy, locally grown foods has increased in the past decade.) I tried all sorts of sprouts and mushrooms and was introduced to the strangeness that is kohlrabi. It was exciting to experiment. I made a lot of mistakes. I still make a lot of mistakes, but that's how I've learned to cook—by reading, watching, and trying over and over again.

After school, I took an internship at a cooking school and bed-and-breakfast in Tuscany. It was there, at Villa Lucia, that I learned a plethora of simple, fresh recipe concepts and also participated in an olive oil harvest. Sunrise to sunset, we handpicked dozens of trees. Believe me, it was not a glamorous job. Eventually I was drawn back home to be with friends, family, and Hugh. At the same time, I was anxious to start a career, even though at the time I had no idea what it would be.

1

I ended up at a few desk jobs, only to figure out that I needed to be around food—to talk about it, to teach people about it, to serve it to people for special occasions, or to use it as a reason to get friends together on a long summer night. I am invested in the emotional connection that comes from cooking and eating. However, it is not just about being fed. Food takes time to plant, grow, transport, and cook, and I always want to be involved with people who value that. I adore the learning, experimenting, sharing, and fulfillment I get from feeding people.

Now here I am, the taquito-eating little girl, sharing seasonal, produce-focused recipes in an attempt to inspire people to eat well.

My husband and I publish Sprouted Kitchen, a whole foods–focused blog for which I make the food and Hugh takes the pictures. We didn't imagine it would be as successful as it's been, but the return on our investment of time has exceeded our expectations. My goal is to share recipes that are simple enough to make after work but interesting enough that you could serve them at a dinner party. I want my recipes to be fresh and light, while always keeping great flavor as the priority.

I am so grateful that my adventures with food include Hugh. I am absolutely enamored with him for a number of reasons, and I am beyond impressed that he has taught himself to take stunning pictures of food. He encourages me to pay closer attention to the aesthetics of a dish while simultaneously convincing me that I know what I am doing . . . even when I burn all the crostini, make cookies that taste like foil, or dump the entire container of salt into the caramelized onions. In those moments, you need someone who loves and believes in you to remind you that you know what you're doing. We make a great team.

My hope is that readers will flip through this book and find a comfortable approach to the kitchen. You may be just learning, or perhaps you have been cooking for sixty-seven years, but I hope that I have included something for everyone. Keep in mind that recipes are often just a starting point, and you may omit or add ingredients according to your preferences. Trust yourself, change things, and make the recipes your own. People who cook well usually use their intuition rather than relying on measurements, so give yourself permission to be creative.

Making fresh food with wholesome seasonal ingredients should help you simplify your time in the kitchen, not complicate it. If I can convince just one reader that making muffins from scratch with whole grains is tastier and more rewarding than buying them from a grocery store, then the value and gratitude that I was shown to feel toward food will have come full circle.

how to read this book

One of the biggest challenges I faced when writing this book was explaining in words the precise details of how to make something, when in fact I don't typically think about cooking in such a way. I wish you could just come over and I would show you! Words can often make easy tasks seem more difficult than they really are, and this book is far from advanced. Read through the recipe first, then go for it, referring to the recipe as necessary.

As I suggested above, you should trust your own intuition. I rarely offer measurements for salt and pepper because I feel everyone has their own preferences. I prefer less salt and tons of pepper, while Hugh likes the opposite, so I found it best to allow people to make that call on their own in most cases. You must taste as you go to figure this out. I would suggest finding a salt that you like and using it consistently. Different types of salt contain different minerals and have a different salinity, so a pinch of one is not always equal to a pinch of another. There are books dedicated to the art of using different salts, and this is not it. I use a fine-grain sea salt or pink salt in everyday cooking, and Maldon sea salt flakes for finishing dishes or sprinkling on top of some sweets.

Do you have the space (and the proper climate) to grow a lemon tree? You should plant one if you do. Fresh citrus juice adds a brightness to food that is unmatched by any vinegar. I consistently use Meyer lemons, which are sweeter and less acidic than standard lemons, because I have access to a tree. You can find Meyer lemons in markets in the winter and spring, but if you have your own tree you'll have access to them for longer, plus you'll save money in the long run. Am I starting off my book by suggesting you plant a tree? Why yes, yes I am. And an herb garden while you're at it. You'll thank me later.

We get the majority of our produce from a CSA program, which is basically a subscription to a farm. For our weekly payment we get a box of whatever happens to be in season. Because the box is limited to what is bountiful at that farm at that time, and often there are weeks when we get a *lot* of Swiss chard, I fill in the gaps at a farmers' market or a grocery store that has a lot of organic options and a high turnover rate. This also gives me the chance to stock up on grains and flours from bulk bins, which tend to be more affordable than packaged goods. Your produce doesn't have to be expensive, but you can usually tell by looking at it if it is "happy." Is it firm, bright, and fragrant? Then it's probably happy.

Where my food comes from and how it is grown is important to me. Even if you do not care about the politics of sustainable agriculture, the flavor of your food will be indescribably better when you cook food that is fresh and in season. Research what foods are in season in your area, and discover which markets sell them, and you will be certain to make good food because you started with good food.

There are a few terms in this book that are vague for good reason, but I respect that there are some cooks who like specifics. Here's what I mean when you see the following:

Handful = short of $1/4$ cup
Pinch = a bit less than $1/2$ teaspoon
Heaping = a bit more than the measurement
Scant = just short of the measurement

This should be fun. Trust yourself. Find good company. Meyer lemons. Lots of herbs. Salt + pepper. Be well.

ingredients and tools

the pantry: flours, sweeteners, and oils

Hugh and I are lucky to live in a place with a generous amount of pantry and cupboard space. Before that, however, I'd spent years living in a small studio or sharing a kitchen with roommates, where space was limited; so when we moved into our current home, I took full advantage of the opportunity to fill our shelves with grains, flours, sweeteners, and oils that I knew I would use. Stocking a variety of items in your pantry will provide opportunities to be creative, as well as leave you the option of using fewer processed staples. A few of these items may not be available in conventional markets, but they can be purchased at larger natural foods stores like Whole Foods or purchased online.

FLOURS

When you consider substituting one flour for another, keep in mind the protein content of each, especially if they lack gluten. Less gluten will result in a lighter, crumbly baked good, while more can help a yeasted bread rise or make pizza dough more elastic. When I am doing gluten-free baking, I don't use added gums, as some cooks do, as my ratios of flour to protein (eggs, most often) are adjusted so that the baked good, although it might be delicate, will stay together.

Almond Meal

Nut meal and nut flour are both made of ground nuts. A nut flour, which typically costs more, is usually made from a blanched nut, and some purists consider it to have a more refined flavor. The recipes in this book call for almond meal, which is not blanched. I buy mine at Trader Joe's or make my own when I buy almonds in bulk; all it takes is a quick whirl in the food processor. It is a gluten-free, higher-protein, and lower-carbohydrate alternative to wheat flours but tends to make baked goods drier and quite delicate. If you don't use it often, it keeps for up to eight months stored in the fridge.

Gluten-Free All-Purpose Flour

There are a number of books and online resources that can assist you in combining your own flours to create a gluten-free blend, but for the few times I use it, I like Bob's Red Mill brand just fine. It is a mix of garbanzo flour, potato starch, and tapioca flour along with a few other things. A number of its ingredients are expensive to buy on their own if you don't use them often. For my cornmeal pancakes, I offer the option of making them gluten free by balancing the cornmeal with this flour to smooth out the texture. This flour does not yield the same exact results as all-purpose flour, but it's quite convenient for those with a gluten intolerance.

Spelt Flour

This whole grain flour has a barely sweet, toasty, and nutty flavor. It is similar in taste to whole wheat flour, but it is made from a grain with a tougher outer shell. It has slightly more protein than whole wheat flour. It is an option for those on a wheat-free diet but is not completely gluten free. If you are using it in place of all-purpose flour in your favorite recipe, start off by substituting just half of the regular flour with spelt, as the results can be a bit heavy.

Whole Wheat Pastry Flour

This is my most frequently used flour. Typically ground from soft white wheat, it results in a more tender product than does regular whole wheat flour, which is milled from hard red wheat and contains a bit more protein (14 percent versus 9 percent, on average). I bake more cookies and cakes than I do bread and pizza dough, so this is a staple in my kitchen.

Unbleached All-Purpose Flour or Unbleached White Whole Wheat Flour

There are some moments when you just need a basic all-purpose flour with a fairly neutral flavor. The former is the closest thing you'll find to white flour in this book, and I use it infrequently, but sometimes it's necessary (for example, when making shortbread!). Unbleached white whole wheat flour has a slightly nuttier wheat flavor and a bit more nutritional value, being milled from hard white spring wheat. A "real" baker would tell you that they are not equals in a recipe, but I like to live on the edge, so use whichever you keep in your pantry interchangeably here.

SWEETENERS

There is a gamut of sweeteners available to you, each with a different flavor, moisture content, and nutritional content. Though they all contribute sweetness to a recipe, they cannot be substituted for each other without adjustment. As a very general rule, if you want to use a liquid sweetener instead of a dry, you need to scale back the moisture in the recipe by 1/3 or add 1/4 cup of flour to compensate. If you want to use a dry instead of a liquid sweetener, cup for cup, add 1/3 cup more liquid to the recipe.

Agave Nectar

This liquid sweetener comes from the agave plant. It has a lower glycemic index than honey and most dry sugars, but it does have a very high concentration of fructose, hence the differing opinions on whether or not it is better for you than the others. It dissolves in liquid more easily than honey, which makes it the perfect sweetener for dressings, iced tea, and cocktails. I usually use the lighter variety, as the raw or amber agave, which is less filtered, has a caramel or toffee flavor, and when I want that, I reach for real maple syrup.

Brown Rice Syrup

This sweetener is made from fermented brown rice that is heated to make a thick syrup. It is a complex sugar, which means that it is broken down and absorbed into the blood-stream more slowly than most other sweeteners. I use it in granola bars (page 154) and frozen yogurt (page 222), but I have heard it's also a great sweetener for coffee due to its mild flavor and how well it distributes in the hot liquid.

Honey

I prefer to use honey, with its mild floral notes, when I want a spring-tasting sweetness for a fruit dessert or for pairing with a tangy Gorgonzola. I do my best to purchase local honey from the farmers' market, so that I can support the beekeepers whose work is crucial for our food system. There are antioxidants, vitamins, and minerals in honey that you can't get from other sweeteners. If you find honey that has been produced without being heated, more of these benefits stay intact.

Maple Syrup

This is another liquid sweetener with a number of antioxidants, giving it some nutritional value. Maple has a similar caloric content to natural cane sugar, but it has significant amounts of zinc and manganese, which you won't find in other sweeteners. Though the flavor of pure maple syrup is fairly pronounced, I find that the taste mellows out quite a bit when baked. I use it in my Zucchini Bread Bites (page 158) and barely taste the smoky maple flavor. Typically produced in Canada or Vermont, maple syrup is sold in different grades. Grade A has a mild flavor and light color, while Grade B has a stronger maple flavor and deep amber color. Which one you use is typically a matter of personal preference.

Muscovado

Though it is somewhat difficult to find, I use this sweetener often. You should be able to find it at a natural or specialty foods store or on Amazon. It is an unrefined brown sugar that you can buy in both light and dark varieties. It is similar to, yet has a slightly deeper flavor than, your usual brown sugar. Most brown sugar is processed using molasses, while muscovado retains its dark sugarcane juice, which lends a caramel flavor to baked goods and a bit of chew to cookies. Just like brown sugar, it's really moist, so keep it in an airtight container to prevent it from hardening. Any of the recipes that call for muscovado will work fine with regular brown sugar as well. Although muscovado has a slightly higher moisture content, it's not enough to throw off a recipe completely.

Natural Cane Sugar

This category actually encompasses a number of different sweeteners, including Sucanat, demerara, turbinado, and muscovado, as well as a few other sugars that are more difficult to find. When listed in a recipe in this book, it refers to evaporated cane juice that is sometimes labeled as "organic cane sugar" or "natural cane sugar." It is a light beige color as opposed to the bright white of granulated sugar. The closest thing to granulated sugar of all the sweeteners used in this book, it is pretty easy to find in mainstream grocery stores now.

Sucanat

Made by simply crushing fresh-cut sugarcane, extracting the juice, and then dehydrating it, Sucanat has a dry, sandlike texture. Due to this process, it retains any iron, potassium, vitamins, and minerals you would get from sugarcane. It retains its natural molasses and has a faint smokiness to it, so I like to use it in savory rubs and sauces. It can be substituted for white or brown sugar, although the texture is drier and more granular. You might want to add an extra tablespoon or two of liquid to your recipe when using Sucanat.

Turbinado

This coarse sugar is from the first press of the sugarcane, so it retains some of its molasses and nutrition and has a slight caramel flavor. It is sometimes known as Sugar in the Raw, one of the brand names under which it is sold. It does not dissolve as well as other dry sweeteners, so I use it in places where its crunch is appreciated, such as on top of cookies and scones or on the rim of a grapefruit margarita glass.

OILS & FATS

Although "fat" now seems to be considered a bad word, it is a critical component in cooking. Fat is what gives you a smooth mouthfeel, makes cheese melt, locks in the flavors while roasting, and keeps baked goods moist. Most of the ingredients below are used in moderation in this book, but they are crucial to tasty and healthful cooking. Have you ever heard someone rave about a bowl of steamed broccoli with nothing on it? Good oils and fats keep your cells and organs functioning and aid in the absorption of nutrients into the body. Every now and then I'll pick up a unique nut or seed oil, but the following are the fats I use most often. Any nut or seed oil should be kept in the fridge to keep it fresh longer.

Extra-Virgin Coconut Oil

I use this for high-heat cooking in place of canola oil. I am a fan of coconut oil, as it works a lot like butter in baking and cooking. It imparts a richness to cookies and tart crusts while being dairy free and easier to digest than butter. Though it is a saturated fat, it's ideal for those with dairy allergies, as you can use it for savory or sweet applications. Some people say they taste or smell a bit of coconut when it warms, but I really have to put my nose in it to get that. It has a subtle sweetness, but not enough to distract from savory foods. It is a solid at room temperature but melts quickly. I use it primarily for baking, but I love it for roasting squash and root vegetables as well.

Extra-Virgin Olive Oil

Without a question, this is the oil I use most often. With the exception of very high-heat cooking (which compromises the delicate flavor and nutrition of this type of oil) and some baking, it's my all-purpose oil. The words you want on your bottle are "extra-virgin" and "first cold press," and there should be nothing else added. I watched the first press of olives just picked when I lived in Italy, and the liquid comes out from the press an incredible neon green. (If I wasn't embarrassed about my frizzy hair, fur-hooded jacket, and the quality of my point-and-shoot camera, I would show you a picture.)

I keep two bottles of olive oil around. One is a nicer, slightly pricier bottle that I use for dipping bread, dressing salads, and finishing dishes. It's hard for me to suggest a certain brand, as I've tried quite a few that I really like. Although cost is not always related to quality, I do think the herbal grassiness comes through in my more expensive bottle, so I am stingy with that one. The other bottle, which I use more frequently and costs around $10, serves me quite well for day-to-day cooking—coating pans, making baked goods, and whatnot.

Hazelnut and Walnut Oil

These nut oils are strictly finishing oils in my kitchen. I'll drizzle one of them over some roasted vegetables or use it in vinaigrette to dress a vegetable or grain salad, where I appreciate its smooth, nutty flavor. Hazelnut or walnut oil would also be a nice touch to finish a flatbread pizza. Once you taste them, you'll know where to sneak them in as an accent to foods that are delicate, sweet, and earthy.

Organic Unsalted Butter

While I do attempt to keep my use of saturated fats to a minimum, I have no qualms about using butter, cream, or cheese in whole foods–centric cooking. Although a diet high in these ingredients can be harmful to your health, in moderation they can be a part of everyday healthy cooking. After reading all sorts of articles and food documentaries, I make every effort to use organic dairy, although it is difficult with certain types of cheese. There are a few recipes in this book, like the Roasted Cauliflower Capellini (page 104) and the Chocolate-Drizzled Oatmeal Shortbread (page 204), in which the butter contributes to the flavor. However, as a general rule, you can use a scant measurement less coconut oil as a substitute for butter.

While butter can stand fairly high temperatures, the milk solids will burn when exposed to the heat for too long. The solution to this is using ghee or clarified butter, which is unsalted butter that has been heated to separate and remove the butterfat and milk solids. Often people who are lactose intolerant can cook and eat with clarified butter, since the lactose has been removed. Ghee tastes a bit like browned butter, with a nutty aroma, and it's easy to make at home.

Toasted Sesame Oil

The most fragrant of the oils I use, toasted sesame oil packs a lot of flavor. Because it is made from seeds that are already toasted, it doesn't keep the integrity of its flavor when used over high heat or it is cooked for too long. It's ideal for a quick tofu stir-fry or dressing, so you can take advantage of that deep, toasty flavor.

the fridge: eggs and proteins

A majority of the recipes in this book are vegetarian, as a diet rich in produce is a healthy and sustainable way of cooking that I want to encourage. I eat a vegetarian diet with a few sustainable seafood options on occasion, my husband eats everything, and I plan to let my kids make their own decision. I don't draw a hard line and suggest that the choices I make are right for everyone, but I do believe that you are responsible for making wise choices in the proteins you do choose to eat. There are a handful of fish and poultry dishes in this book, and occasionally I suggest using a little bacon, since I love cooking for other people and most people are not vegetarians. You can easily alter the recipes to your liking—bacon lover or not.

EGGS

One of my top five favorite foods, eggs are involved in at least one of my meals daily. They are full of protein and good fats and, given the variety of ways they can be prepared, they can sneak their way gracefully into a plethora of meals. They last a while, are relatively inexpensive, and easy to get your hands on. At the start of each week, I usually pick up a dozen at the farm or farmers' market, and I choose a cage-free organic option at the market when I need more during the week. The disappointing reality about purchasing eggs, however, is that there is vague labeling accountability in this industry. Produce farmers have to pay big money to be qualified as organic and to have that label on their products, but the standards are not nearly as rigorous for eggs. The best way to know you're getting good eggs is to know the farmer or have a trustworthy connection to someone who takes care of the chickens and understands their treatment. As for the regular markets, regardless of the loose rules, I like to think the best of people and assume that if the label says "cage free" (which refers to how the chickens live) and "organic" (which indicates what the chickens are fed), then that is what is in the carton.

Some of the recipes in this book include raw eggs. When eggs are consumed raw, there is always the risk that you will be exposed to bacteria, which are killed by proper cooking. For this reason, when serving food containing raw eggs, always buy certified salmonella-free eggs from a reliable grocer and store them in the refrigerator until you prepare them.

DAIRY

Today you can easily find hormone-free milk, butter, and yogurt, which is labeled as such. You can also find organic options at both conventional and natural foods stores. I suggest buying these, if you can. My old-school father would argue that such labeling is entirely a marketing ploy, and perhaps you know somebody like that (or maybe you are that person!), but I tend to disagree. The cleaner the foods we put in, the better, in my opinion. I've noticed a definitive difference in the taste, too.

FISH AND CHICKEN

I am a big proponent of using the Monterey Bay Aquarium Seafood Watch list when making seafood choices. This ever-changing list tells you which seafood to avoid and which is best to purchase. They have an app for smartphones, too, so I can take the list with me to the market. Look for labels telling you where the seafood is from, since this matters as well, as the list will tell you. Seriously, it's the greatest thing.

When it comes to purchasing poultry, buying organic, free-range options comes with a higher price tag, unfortunately. However, between watching documentaries like *Food, Inc.* and reading a number of articles about the lack of quality and humane practice in raising chickens, I can't bring myself to buy conventional chickens anymore. Just like dairy, the cleaner the better, in my humble opinion.

tools

I've collected a number of kitchen tools and appliances over the years. Some I use frequently, while others just take up space waiting for the one day I may need them. Below is a list of my favorite items that make my time cooking more efficient and enjoyable. It is not lost on me that a few of these things are somewhat pricey, but I believe it is money well spent if you're going to be cooking often.

CAST-IRON SKILLET

Cast-iron skillets often come preseasoned now, which is what makes them somewhat nonstick. They also sear foods beautifully and are ovenproof, so this versatile pan does a little bit of everything. I would say a 10- or 12-inch skillet is the perfect size, depending on how many you typically cook for. If it is not preseasoned, simply cook with a bit of extra oil when first using it to lubricate the pan, or rub it with a neutral oil and put it in a hot oven for an hour before using it. You can bake cornbread or a sturdy cake in it, and it works great for a frittata or anything that requires an even distribution of heat. Don't wash it with soap, as that cuts through the seasoning; just wash it with warm water after cooking and give it a little scrub. If things start to stick, you can use some coarse salt as an abrasive and a teensy bit of soap, if you're feeling paranoid. Take care of it and it will last a lifetime, which is why you can often find them in secondhand stores.

CHEF'S KNIFE

I own five good knives, and I have never once wished that I had more than that. A 7-inch chef's knife is one I would spend a bit more money on, as you'll get great use out of it. It should feel heavy and comfortable to hold. If you take care of your knives, they can last decades. Keep them clean and dry, never put them in the dishwasher, and sharpen them when you start to feel resistance when cutting. The knife should be working for you.

ENAMELED DUTCH OVEN

This item is an investment, as one of decent size and good quality will cost you, but they are a dream to work with. It is essential for cooking the "no knead bread" that is popular these days, allows you to make amazing soups and braises, and cooks a great pot of beans. They are made of enameled cast iron, so you get the benefit of even heat distribution, and they are sturdy enough to remain in the oven for long periods of time. The enamel coating acts as a nonstick surface, and the heavy lid holds in the heat and moisture. Both Staub and Le Creuset make beautiful products with a great reputation.

FOOD PROCESSOR

My life in the kitchen did not begin until I owned a food processor. I was making pestos and hummus in a blender or a Magic Bullet (which I also adore for other uses) for years before I got this baby—and condiments finally became easy to make. It's a pain to clean, and it takes a lot of room to store the large ones, but if my kitchen went up in flames, I would grab my 12-cup Cuisinart before heading out the door. I won't go so far as to say that you need one this big, but it's better to have a bit of extra space in the food processor rather than overpacking a small one.

GRADUATED GLASS BOWLS

There are a few reasons I prefer glass bowls to metal ones. First off, in a pinch, they work perfectly fine as serving bowls. So if I make guacamole in a glass bowl and don't have time to transfer it to a serving dish or I don't want to dirty another bowl, it doesn't look tacky. The heat-proof Pyrex bowls are nonreactive, dishwasher friendly, inexpensive, and microwave-safe, and they coordinate with every color, so my kitchen doesn't end up looking like a hodgepodge mess.

HEATPROOF TONGS

I have far too many burn marks on my hands from picking up things that were clearly too hot for bare hands. Sure, there are oven mitts and dish towels, but having tongs is like having burn-proof fingers. Whether you are grilling, flipping tortillas on the stove, or grabbing a head of roasted garlic or an acorn squash from the oven, they're essential. It seems a silly thing to recommend, I know, but they are constantly in my sink to be washed, so I know they get used all the time. I have two sizes of the OXO Good Grips tongs and they've held up great.

MICROPLANE ZESTER

Upon careful observation, you'll notice that about 70 percent of the recipes in this book call for lemon zest or juice. Using a Microplane zester is more efficient than using the small holes on a box grater, where the zest tends to stick. As essential as it is for zesting citrus, it is just as wonderful for creating fresh grated nutmeg, a sprinkle of Parmesan, or a fine dusting of chocolate to top off a cupcake.

MINI BLENDER

In our house this tool gets its exercise from making protein shakes, smoothies, salad dressings, and mini batches of pesto. I imagine it would also be great for pureeing small batches of steamed veggies for homemade baby food. It is strong for its size and comes with a few different blades and cups in different sizes, so you can change them depending on what you're using it for. The cups are plastic, which makes it great for taking a smoothie with you as you're heading out the door.

PARING KNIFE

For a few years I lived in a teensy studio where the kitchen was actually smaller than the bathroom. I did most of my cooking with a paring knife and a toaster oven and never really felt like I was missing out (although when you're cooking for just yourself there is far less to fuss over). I am usually a proponent of quality over quantity, but a paring knife shouldn't be a big expense. Put your money toward a great chef's knife or serrated knife, but the paring knife has to make it on this list for my frequent use of it. You can take the girl out of the micro kitchen, but can't take the paring knife habit out of the girl.

RIMMED BAKING SHEETS

These also go by the name "jelly roll pans," but I don't know the last time that I, or anyone I know, has made a jelly roll. Maybe you make jelly rolls? This makes the pan even more versatile! I do roast a lot of vegetables, so my rimmed baking sheets are put to good use. There are nonstick types available, but they get stained and scarred just like the regular kinds, and you have to be extra careful when using them, so I typically buy ones made out of heavy-duty aluminum or steel. I have a small one for toasting nuts and a few larger ones for vegetables, baking, and whatnot. The heavier ones are a tad more expensive, but they won't warp in the hot oven and they last forever. The kitchenware store Sur La Table carries a few really nice ones, and they are also easy to find at restaurant supply stores.

meal ideas

I put together a few menus for occasions that may bring you to the kitchen. I like to eat good food, but I find it so much more enjoyable with good company. My intention here is to offer you some suggestions for recipes that may work well together for different circumstances. For breakfast I try to offer both a savory and a sweet, or for a dinner outside I include some dishes that are served well family-style. Take it, leave it, or change things around however works best for you.

A BRUNCH WITH FRIENDS
multigrain carrot-date muffins
ranchero breakfast tostadas
mango mint lassi

A SLOW SUNDAY MORNING AT HOME
french press coffee
pumpkin pecan granola
soft scrambled eggs with creamy leeks

A WEEKDAY LUNCH
roasted tomato soup
toasted millet salad with arugula, quick pickled onions, and goat cheese
almond meal cookies with coconut and cacao nibs

MAKE-AHEAD SNACKS FOR HOUSEGUESTS
quinoa collard wraps with miso-carrot spread
toasty nuts
zucchini bread bites
mango guacamole and baked corn chips

A CASUAL DINNER FOR GUESTS
white sangria
beer bean– and cotija-stuffed poblanos
papaya and red quinoa salad with mexican caesar dressing
coconut lime tart

A LIGHTER "COMFORT FOOD" MEAL
braised white beans and leeks
brussel leaf and baby spinach sauté
roasted wild cod with meyer lemon and caper relish
inside-out apple pie à la mode

DINING AL FRESCO
honey mustard broccoli salad
spiced sweet potato wedges
chipotle and apple turkey burgers
oatmeal ice cream sandwiches

HAPPY HOUR WITH THE GIRLS
grapefruit margarita
lemon and herb hummus
polenta squares with raw corn and blueberry relish
tofu summer rolls with cashew dipping sauce
flourless chocolate-banana pudding cakes with cinnamon cream

A ROMANTIC NIGHT IN
heirloom tomato stacks with bocconcini and kale pesto
roasted cauliflower capellini
grilled peaches with maple crème fraîche

To Start the Morning

I can remember waking up to the smell of bacon on weekends as a kid. My dad, who was used to waking up for work, would get up early and be finished eating breakfast and reading the paper before the rest of us came downstairs. My mom would make us this icy drink with frozen orange juice concentrate, vanilla, and milk while my sister and I sat at the counter begging for just one spoonful of the concentrate. We thought that stuff was so delicious! My dad finished more than half the bacon on his own before we ever got to the table, but he made up for it by making our eggs to order: scrambled for my sister and me and sunny-side up for my mom. It was simple. Eggs, bacon, and toast. And although my breakfast preferences have changed over time, I hope to always honor that time, as there is absolutely nothing like enjoying a nice warm breakfast before the day has a chance to get to you.

That said, breakfast means a lot of different things to different people, and your story is different than mine. Maybe you rush out of the house in the morning and need something quick, like a smoothie or a muffin from a batch you made over the weekend. Or, if the morning is your quiet time before the day gets going, perhaps good coffee and a savory scramble is your peace. This chapter feeds each of these needs, offering a few things that can be made in advance, and a couple that take more time and would make a nice brunch on a slow Sunday. There are both savory and sweet options, some dishes that are quick and others that are more involved, but in any case, these recipes should start your morning on a good note.

roasted tomato and
herb omelette

SERVES 2 <

2 cups baby tomatoes

2 teaspoons extra-virgin olive oil

1/2 teaspoon garlic salt

2 tablespoons chopped fresh flat-leaf
parsley

5 eggs

2 tablespoons whole milk or cream

Pinch of sea salt

2 teaspoons unsalted butter

1/3 cup shredded Jack cheese

1/4 cup chopped fresh basil, plus more
for garnish

Freshly ground pepper

Preheat the oven to 350°F. Line a rimmed baking sheet with parchment paper. Halve the tomatoes and spread them on the baking
sheet. Drizzle the oil and sprinkle the garlic salt and parsley on top of
the tomatoes and toss to coat. Spread them out in an even layer and
bake until they are slightly dried and shriveled at the edges, about
30 minutes. Remove from the oven and let cool.

In a bowl, whisk together the eggs, milk, and salt until the mixture
is a uniform color. In an 8-inch nonstick pan, heat 1 teaspoon of the
butter over medium heat and swirl to coat the pan. Add half of the egg
mixture to the pan and quickly tilt the pan so that the egg mixture
covers the bottom. When the bottom of the egg mixture starts to set,
turn the heat down to low. Use a silicone spatula to push the cooked
edges toward the center of the pan, sweeping along the outer edge of
the omelette and lifting the cooked eggs to allow the uncooked egg
to run beneath them. When the omelette is set on the bottom, put
a handful of the roasted tomatoes on one-third of the omelette and
sprinkle half of the cheese and basil on top of the tomatoes. Fold the
omelette into thirds, like a letter, and slide it onto a plate. Don't fret
if the center is a bit underdone; it will continue to cook once folded.
Repeat with the remaining ingredients to make a second omelette.

Garnish each omelette with more basil and the pepper and serve.

Making an omelette

is pretty straightforward, though it
takes a bit of practice to get a pretty
one. Still, even an imperfect omelette
tastes great. I'm charmed by the Julia
Child method of just vigorously shaking a hot pan until the eggs fold into
themselves, but that doesn't work
when you use a filling, as you do here.

The tastiest part about this dish is
the slow-roasted tomatoes, which
shrink down and leave you with sweet,
deeply flavored, and just slightly tangy
gems. I usually double or triple the
roasted tomatoes so that I have extras
to throw on salads or have around for
the next time I'm craving an omelette.
If you aren't much for Jack cheese, a
nice white Cheddar or soft goat cheese
would be great too. You can make the
roasted tomatoes the night before and
keep them covered in the fridge, but
be sure to bring them to room temperature before starting the eggs.

quick apricot jam

1 1/2 pounds ripe apricots

2 tablespoons freshly squeezed orange juice

1/3 to 2/3 cup natural cane sugar

Pinch of sea salt

Cut the apricots in half (or in quarters if they are on the larger side) and discard the pits. You can leave the skin on; it will break down when the apricots are cooked.

In a large, heavy pot over medium heat, combine the apricots, orange juice, and 1/3 cup of the sugar and stir. Once the mixture is warmed through and the juices start to release, add the salt and turn the heat up to medium-high. Continue to cook, stirring frequently with a wooden spoon, until the fruit breaks down and resembles a puree, about 15 minutes. Taste for sweetness and add more of the sugar, if necessary. When the jam reads 190°F to 200°F on a candy thermometer, remove the jam from the heat and transfer to a bowl to stop the cooking process. Give it a few more stirs to release the steam and allow it to cool completely. Use at once or transfer the jam to a clean glass jar and keep it in the fridge for up to 2 weeks.

There are people who are serious about making jam, using pectin, doing freezer tests to dial in the perfect consistency, and whatnot. I really admire people who pay that much attention to detail, and there is a craft to making the perfect jam—but when you find yourself with an abundance of summer apricots, it doesn't get any easier than this unfussy version. It's the perfect spread for some fresh toasty bread. I'm also hooked on apricot jam and Manchego grilled cheese sandwiches. If you make this jam, you really must try that combination. It's dreamy.

This jam can vary a lot in sweetness, depending on how ripe your apricots are. Fruit that ripens on the tree always tastes best, so find a market or farmer that sells fragrant, slightly soft apricots. Making this jam with very ripe fruit will allow you to use less sugar without it being too tart.

french press coffee

SERVES 2 <

825 grams (about 3 1/2 cups) cold filtered water

55 grams (about 1/2 cup) coffee beans

In a kettle, heat the water; the target temperature is just a touch over 200°F. Fill a French press coffeepot with hot tap water; otherwise, the pot will rob a significant amount of heat from your water when you begin to brew, resulting in underextracted coffee.

Measure out the beans. I use a 15:1 water-to-bean ratio, so for Sara and me I use 825 grams of water and 55 grams of beans. You'll need to experiment a bit with grinding the beans. The rule of thumb is that you want the grind about the coarseness of sea salt. This is where the quality of your grinder comes into play. A high-quality grinder will yield a more uniform grind. A poor grinder will grind most of the coffee properly but will yield too-fine grinds that will overextract during the brewing process as well as overly coarse grinds that will underextract.

Pour the tap water out of the French press pot. Put the pot on your food scale, add the coffee grounds, and zero out the scale.

Add 200 grams of 200°F water to the pot and use a spoon to agitate the water-coffee mixture as little as possible while still ensuring all the grounds are fully saturated. Now start a timer. If you're using fresh beans you'll see the mixture "bloom."

At 0:45 on the timer, use the spoon to break the crust and to deflate the bloom so that all the grinds settle back into the slurry, still agitating them as little as possible. Add the additional 625 grams of water, stir gently, and place the lid on the press.

I am particular about

a few things, such as tidiness, being on time, and returning emails, while Hugh has selective obsessive compulsiveness that only shows through on the things he really cares about. He has taken to the craft of coffee with a bit of that obsessiveness, and I am lucky to be the beneficiary. Though using a French press is not Hugh's preferred method at the moment, it is the tool that many people have on hand. According to Hugh, there are four major variables in this method: the water temperature, the water-to-coffee ratio, the coarseness of the grind, and the brewing duration. These directions yield a cup that Hugh and I both really like, but if you want something a little different, tweak one or more of those variables until you find what you're looking for. The following are his directions. Some of you will love them, and the others will find him completely nuts. Note that it's helpful to use a food scale to measure the water and beans in grams for this recipe.

At 3:30, gently stir the mixture once more. You'll see a light brown foamy layer resting on top of the liquid; these are the fines. Scoop most of the fines out with your spoon and discard; you may have to sacrifice a bit of the liquid, but tallyho. At 4:00, replace the lid, press the plunger, and pour. Don't empty the last bit into your cups; nobody likes the dregs.

ranchero breakfast tostadas

SERVES 4 <

BLACK BEAN MASH

2 cups cooked black beans

1/4 to 1/2 cup light sour cream

2 green onions, white and green parts, chopped

1 teaspoon ground cumin

1/2 teaspoon sea salt

1 teaspoon freshly ground pepper

4 slices cooked bacon, chopped (optional)

8 small corn tortillas

Extra-virgin olive oil, for brushing

1 tablespoon coconut oil or unsalted butter

8 eggs

1 cup shredded white Cheddar cheese

2 avocados, peeled and thinly sliced

1/3 cup chopped fresh cilantro

1 lime, in wedges

Hot sauce, for serving (optional)

Whether cooking the beans from scratch or using canned, drain the beans and add them to a saucepan over low heat and warm through. Add about 1/4 cup tepid water, 1/4 cup of the sour cream, the green onions, cumin, salt, and pepper and mash with a potato masher or a large fork until coarsely mashed but not entirely smooth. Stir in the bacon. Taste for salt and pepper, add the remaining sour cream if you'd like the beans to be creamier, then turn off the heat and keep covered until needed.

Preheat the oven to 400°F. Brush the tops of the tortillas with a bit of olive oil and lay them on a rimmed baking sheet (it's fine if they overlap). Bake until just lightly browned, 6 to 8 minutes. Remove from the oven and set aside.

Heat a large frying pan with the coconut oil over medium heat. Working in batches as necessary, gently break the eggs in the pan and cook sunny-side up or to your desired doneness, covering the pan if you like your yolks more cooked through. Build a tostada by topping a tortilla with about 1/4 cup of the bean mash, 1 egg, and an eighth of the cheese, avocado slices, and cilantro. Repeat with the remaining ingredients. Serve garnished with a slice of lime and hot sauce to taste.

This is my version of huevos rancheros, which I make for weekend breakfast or brunch when I want to serve something on the filling side. We have breakfast for dinner some week-nights, and this is also perfect for that. Making the bean mash from scratch is the only time-consuming part, but you could save time by using canned beans, or you can make the beans the night before so they're ready in the morning. Reheat the beans with a bit of warm water to loosen them. I make these with a fried egg, but a poached or scrambled egg would work just as well.

vegetable eggs benedict

SERVES 2 <

3 to 4 ounces soft goat cheese

1/4 cup whole milk, slightly warmed

1 1/4 cups roasted bell peppers,
    chopped

1 tablespoon freshly squeezed lemon
    juice

1 tablespoon Dijon mustard

Splash of hot sauce

Sea salt and freshly ground pepper

12 asparagus spears, trimmed

1 tablespoon extra-virgin olive oil

1/2 teaspoon garlic salt

Grated zest of 1 lemon

5 cups fresh spinach leaves

4 cups water

1 tablespoon red wine or apple cider
    vinegar

4 eggs

2 whole grain English muffins

Arrange a rack in the upper third of your oven and preheat the oven
to 500°F.

In a blender or food processor, combine the goat cheese, milk, roasted
peppers, lemon juice, mustard, hot sauce, and a pinch of salt and
blend until smooth. Cover and set aside.

Toss the asparagus with 1/2 tablespoon of the olive oil, the garlic salt,
and a pinch or two of pepper. Spread across a baking sheet and bake
until slightly blistered, about 8 minutes, depending on the thickness
of the spears.

Warm the remaining 1/2 tablespoon olive oil in a sauté pan over
medium heat. Add the lemon zest, a pinch of salt and pepper, and the
spinach and sauté until just wilted, about 1 minute. Turn off the heat
and leave the mixture in the pan.

To poach the eggs, in a saucepan, bring the water and vinegar to a boil
over high heat, then turn the heat down to a very gentle boil. Break
1 of the eggs into a small ramekin and gently slip it into the water.
Repeat with 1 more of the eggs. The white of the egg will spread a

(continued)

There seems to be some-
thing so daring about a poached egg:
with its decadent runny yolk, it seems
to add sophistication to a simple dish
and makes it more of a meal. The truth
is, however, I'm a scrambled lady to
the bone, except for in a few dishes,
and this recipe is one of them. I think
it's because I adore the sauce, and
once you dig in with your fork and the
beautiful stack becomes a bit dishev-
eled, the runny yolk makes the sauce
even thicker and richer. So I assure you
that if you are in the scrambled egg
camp with me, this is the time to test
the waters.

When the sauce is made with roasted
yellow bell peppers, it resembles hol-
landaise. Using jarred roasted peppers
will save you time, but be sure to drain
them well. If you don't care for goat
cheese, you could use cream cheese or
ricotta instead.

This is meant for two hungry people,
but if you're serving some sides—
maybe a nice fruit salad—it could
serve as a very light breakfast for four.

bit, but just push it back toward the yolk with a spoon. Poach until they reach the desired doneness, 1 to 2 minutes, then remove with a slotted spoon. Keep warm in a bowl of warm water while you repeat with the remaining 2 eggs.

Toast the English muffins and get ready to layer. Arrange two muffin halves on a plate and top with a spoonful of the sauce, half of the sautéed spinach, half of the asparagus spears, 2 of the poached eggs, and another spoonful of the sauce. Repeat with the remaining ingredients and serve warm.

soft scrambled eggs with creamy leeks

SERVES 4 <

10 eggs

6 tablespoons whole milk

3 large leeks, white and light green parts, cleaned

1 tablespoon unsalted butter

Sea salt and freshly ground pepper

2 teaspoons coarsely chopped fresh thyme or tarragon leaves, plus more for garnish

1 tablespoon extra-virgin olive oil

In a large mixing bowl, whisk together the eggs and 2 tablespoons of the milk until light and evenly mixed. You will feel a resistance when you start whisking the eggs, but when they are fully combined, that resistance will give. Set aside.

Halve the leeks lengthwise and slice into thin half moons. Warm the butter in a large sauté pan over medium heat. Add the leeks and $1/2$ teaspoon of salt and stir to coat. Sauté, stirring occasionally, until the leeks are softened and browned in parts, 12 to 15 minutes. Add

All scrambled eggs are not created equal: the temperature of the eggs and pan, the addition of milk or cream, and how much you stir them all make a big difference. Hugh has mastered scrambled eggs, which is actually much less a scramble than it is a gentle push of the eggs toward the center of the pan until they are just barely set in feathered folds of light yellow. When I'm feeling patient, a slow scramble over low heat, stirred frequently almost like a risotto, yields a soft mound of eggs. Hugh's method, an almost omelette-esque approach, is a bit quicker and is used here.

The leeks in this dish are tender from a long sauté in a big pan, while the

the remaining 4 tablespoons of milk and the thyme and cook until the liquid is absorbed into the leeks. Turn off the heat and set aside.

In a large nonstick pan, preferably 12 inches, heat the olive oil over medium-low heat. Give the eggs one more whisk. When the pan is warm, tilt it so the oil puddles in the corner closest to you and slowly pour in the eggs into the center of the oil, so the oil spreads outward with the eggs as you lower the pan down. Cook the eggs without stirring until the bottom just starts to set, then gently push the cooked eggs from the edges of the pan toward the center, letting the uncooked parts fall back toward the edges. Continue until the eggs are almost cooked, turn off the heat, add a pinch or two of salt and pepper and give them another push to make sure any uncooked parts touch the bottom of the pan. Immediately transfer to plates, garnish with more thyme, and serve with the leeks.

butter and milk bring out their natural creaminess. I adore the leeks with eggs, but they are also great with seafood, on top of grilled meats, and mixed into all sorts of noodle and bean dishes. So simple but so perfect!

Even if you reduce the number of eggs to make this dish for fewer people, make the full batch of leeks. Once you have them you'll figure out other places to throw in the leftovers.

I prefer to remove the eggs from the fridge and whisk them before cooking the leeks so the eggs come up in temperature. This makes a difference in the texture, believe it or not. Pull the eggs from the heat before they look completely done, as they'll continue to cook a bit more from the residual heat.

multigrain carrot-date muffins

MAKES 12 SMALL OR 8 LARGE MUFFINS <

1 cup low-fat buttermilk

$^1/_4$ cup unsalted butter, melted and slightly cooled, plus more for the tins

1 egg

1 teaspoon pure vanilla extract

$^1/_4$ cup finely chopped pitted Medjool dates

1$^1/_2$ cups loosely packed grated carrots

$^3/_4$ cup whole wheat pastry flour

$^3/_4$ cup oat bran

$^1/_2$ cup almond meal

$^1/_3$ cup unbleached cake flour

$^1/_2$ cup muscovado sugar

$^1/_3$ cup turbinado sugar, plus more for sprinkling

1 teaspoon baking powder

1 teaspoon baking soda

1 teaspoon ground cinnamon

$^1/_4$ teaspoon ground ginger, optional

$^1/_2$ teaspoon sea salt

Preheat the oven to 350°F.

In a large bowl, whisk together the buttermilk, butter, egg, and vanilla extract until well combined. Add the dates and carrots and set aside. In another mixing bowl, sift the remaining ingredients together, making sure there are no clumps. Gently stir the dry ingredients into the wet until just combined, being careful not to overmix. Let sit for about 5 minutes for the batter to poof up just a bit.

Meanwhile, prepare your muffin tins by lining with paper liners or greasing with a thin layer of butter on all sides. You will get 12 small muffins if you fill a standard muffin tin halfway full, or about 8 larger muffins if you fill them to the brim (these will spill over the top while baking, so grease the top of the tin as well). Sprinkle a bit of extra turbinado sugar on top of each muffin. Bake until the tops of the muffins are just browned and a toothpick inserted into a muffin comes out clean, 21 to 23 minutes for smaller muffins and 25 to 27 minutes for larger ones.

Remove the pan from the oven. When just cool enough to handle, twist each muffin out and turn it on its side to release the steam. Serve warm, or store in an airtight container for 4 to 5 days.

There is no denying that a nice pastry is perfect paired with a hot cup of coffee. My coffee epicure husband always chooses a baked good in the morning for this very reason. This recipe for my go-to muffins is our compromise, because they have a great sweetness from the carrots and dates while also being packed with whole grains. You could even put a bit of maple-sweetened cream cheese on top if you want something more decadent.

This recipe uses a lot of different flours, but if you can find a store with bulk bins, you can purchase just what you need of flours that you don't use often. The oat bran and almond flour are important for the muffins' texture, but you could substitute whole wheat pastry flour for the cake flour or vice versa if you want to reduce the number of ingredients. I use the small holes of a grater to shred the carrots, because it results in carrots that will blend smoothly into the batter rather than remaining chunky. If you let the batter sit a bit after you combine the wet and dry ingredients, the baking powder and soda will have some time to react before they hit the heat, which gives them more leavening power.

pumpkin pecan granola

MAKES ABOUT 3 CUPS <

2 1/2 tablespoons extra-virgin olive oil

Sea salt

3/4 teaspoon pumpkin pie spice

1/3 cup Grade B maple syrup

1/3 cup pumpkin puree

2 cups old-fashioned rolled oats

1/2 cup raw pecan pieces

3 tablespoons sesame seeds

1/2 cup crimson or golden raisins

Preheat the oven to 325°F.

In a large mixing bowl, combine the olive oil, 1/2 teaspoon salt, the pumpkin pie spice, maple syrup, and pumpkin puree and whisk to combine. Add the oats, pecans, and sesame seeds and stir until evenly coated.

Spread the mixture on the baking sheet, keeping some of the clusters of oats and nuts intact so that the finished granola will have some chunks. Bake the granola, stirring every so often by scooping the mixture from the edges of the pan toward the middle and spreading it evenly again, until dry and light brown in color, 35 to 45 minutes. Remove from the oven and allow the granola to cool a few minutes. Add the raisins and toss to mix. Add another pinch or two of salt if needed. Cool completely before storing. Store in an airtight container for up to 2 weeks.

If you've ever made granola at home, you're aware that the store-bought stuff is no comparison. Homemade granola has a fresh crunch, it smells of spices and toasty oats, and the sugar and fat is about half that of the stuff in a box. I've tried a few recipes that called for melted butter to ensure the granola turns crisp, but I've found that olive oil yields the same results. If you're skeptical, I assure you that the flavor of the oil gets lost in the pumpkin and spices.

The ingredients could easily be doubled to make enough to last you through the week—for serving on yogurt, with milk, and for general snacking. Be sure to bake it in a single layer, though, or steam created in the crowded pan will keep the granola from turning crisp.

creamy coconut barley with pomegranate molasses

SERVES 4 <

1¹/₄ cups pearled barley
1 (13.5-ounce) can light coconut milk
¹/₄ teaspoon ground cardamom
Pinch of sea salt

¹/₂ cup shredded coconut, lightly toasted
1 cup pomegranate seeds
¹/₄ cup pomegranate molasses

Rinse the barley in a mesh strainer. Add the barley and 1 cup water to a small saucepan and bring to a simmer over medium heat. When the water is almost absorbed, after about 8 minutes, stir in ¹/₂ cup of the coconut milk and the cardamom. Keep the heat at a gentle simmer and stir occasionally, as if you were cooking risotto. Continue to add the coconut milk, about ¹/₂ cup at a time, until the barley is cooked through but still al dente. If necessary, add a bit more water and continue simmering until it reaches the desired doneness. Stir in the salt.

Divide the barley among 4 bowls and top each serving with the toasted coconut and pomegranate seeds. Add some pomegranate molasses, starting small (it's very sweet) and adding more according to your taste. Serve hot.

Despite the fact that I love to cook, I have been eating the same weekday breakfast for a number of months now: scrambled eggs with greens and a swipe of hummus in a brown rice tortilla. I love it. It fills me up and is sort of a ritual now. I mention this because I know a number of people whose breakfast ritual is a bowl of oatmeal with fruit and nuts, and maybe a bit of maple or cream. There is a homeyness about eating a warm bowl of grains in the morning. I like oatmeal, but I think this combination of creamy coconut, tart pomegranate, and nutty, toothsome barley makes a nice change to a breakfast routine. The barley saves well—you can keep it covered in the fridge for up to 3 days and reheat it with a bit more liquid to loosen it up.

buckwheat crepes with smoked salmon

SERVES 4 <

CREPES

2 cups milk

2 eggs

1 tablespoon natural cane sugar

1 tablespoon unsalted butter, melted and slightly cooled, plus more for the pan

1/2 cup buckwheat flour

1/2 cup unbleached all-purpose flour

1/4 teaspoon sea salt

FILLING

1 1/2 cups small-curd cottage cheese

Grated zest of 1 lemon

1/4 cup chopped fresh chives

Freshly ground pepper

1 tart apple, such as Granny Smith or Pink Lady

6 ounces thinly sliced smoked salmon

To make the crepe batter, combine the milk, eggs, sugar, and butter in a blender and blend until smooth. In a bowl, sift together both flours and the salt and add half the flour mixture to the blender. Give it a few whirls, then add the rest of the flour mixture and blend until smooth. Cover and let rest for 30 minutes, or in the fridge overnight (letting it return to room temperature before cooking).

In a mixing bowl, combine the cottage cheese, lemon zest, chives, and a few grinds of pepper. Stir together. Core the apple and, using a mandoline, if you have one, slice paper-thin.

Place a 10-inch nonstick pan (or a crepe pan, if you're so lucky) over medium heat and rub the bottom with a bit of butter. Pour 1/3 cup of the batter into the pan and quickly swirl it around a few times to coat the bottom of the pan evenly. Cook until it looks dry around the edges, 1 to 2 minutes, then run a silicone spatula around the edge to lift up the crepe and carefully flip it over to cook the other side for 1 minute more.

When I was in France years ago, I noticed that crepes seemed to be the fast food of the country (in a good way). There are nooks in every alleyway where someone stands at a crepe maker, at the ready to pour a bit of fresh batter on the pan and fill it with sweet or savory treats. The crepe, because it is so delicate, begs to be filled delicately. This is not a burrito; don't stuff it full.

It is always best to let the batter rest overnight in the refrigerator and bring it back to room temperature in the morning. You want the batter to be smooth, so if there are still a few clumps after mixing, pass it through a strainer. Although you could make all eight crepes and keep them in a warm oven or under a dish towel until ready to eat, they are amazing straight out of the pan. You may feel like a short-order cook, but this is the way they taste best.

Dislike smoked salmon? Just go with the cottage cheese and apples. Dislike cottage cheese? A bit of crème fraîche or even some smashed avocado is a great alternative. Be creative.

Flip it over one more time, place some of the cottage cheese mixture, a slice of smoked salmon, and a couple of apple slices in the center of the crepe. Fold both sides of the crepe in toward the center and serve warm. Repeat with the remaining ingredients.

cornmeal cakes with cherry compote

SERVES 4 <

CHERRY COMPOTE

1 pound Bing cherries

2 tablespoons fresh thyme leaves

$^1/_4$ cup water

$^1/_3$ cup honey

Pinch of sea salt

PANCAKES

1 cup fine stone-ground cornmeal

2 tablespoons honey, plus more for serving

$1^1/_2$ tablespoons unsalted butter, plus more for the griddle and for serving

$^3/_4$ cup boiling water

$^3/_4$ cup gluten-free all-purpose or white whole wheat flour

1 teaspoon baking soda

1 teaspoon sea salt

3 tablespoons natural cane sugar

$^3/_4$ cup buttermilk

1 egg, beaten

To make the compote, using a paring knife or a cherry pitter, remove the pits from the cherries. Cut the cherries into quarters and put the pieces in a small saucepan. Add the thyme and the water and warm the cherries over medium heat, stirring every so often until they just barely start to break down, about 3 minutes. Stir in the honey and salt, turn off the heat, and set aside. It can be rewarmed after you prepare your pancakes.

To make the pancakes, put the cornmeal, honey, and butter in a large mixing bowl. Pour the boiling water over the cornmeal mixture and stir. Cover the bowl with a dish towel and allow it to sit for 5 minutes to soften the cornmeal.

In another bowl, sift the flour, baking soda, salt, and sugar together. Add the buttermilk and egg to the softened cornmeal mixture and stir to mix completely. Add in the dry ingredients and stir.

Heat your griddle or cast-iron pan over medium heat and rub a bit of butter on the surface. Pour a scant $^1/_4$ cup of the batter onto the griddle,

Though I usually vote for a savory breakfast over a sweet one, the cornmeal here gives these pancakes a substantial texture and keeps them from being too decadent, and the cherries add a nice tartness. These are not frilly pancakes; they are assured in their flavors. Soaking the cornmeal in warm liquid for a bit softens the texture and makes the pancakes more tender, though you still get the slightest bit of that familiar cornmeal crunch.

If you don't eat gluten, whether because of allergies or other reasons, you can use gluten-free flour in this recipe, but white whole wheat flour works great too.

leaving it plenty of space to spread (the batter is pretty thin). Once you start to see little bubbles on the surface, flip the pancake over and cook another 1 to 2 minutes. Repeat with the remaining batter.

You may keep the pancakes warm in a 200°F oven while you finish the batch, or serve immediately with a scoop of the warm cherry compote. Drizzle with a bit of butter and honey to taste.

tofu quiche in rosemary–almond meal crust

SERVES 4 <

CRUST

1 1/2 cups almond meal

1/2 teaspoon sea salt

1 tablespoon finely chopped fresh rosemary

1 tablespoon water

Scant 1/4 cup coconut oil

FILLING

1 (12.3-ounce) package silken tofu, firm

1 tablespoon coconut oil or extra-virgin olive oil

2 cups chopped cremini mushrooms

Salt and freshly ground pepper

1 small yellow onion, thinly sliced

2 tablespoons nutritional yeast

1 tablespoon tahini

2 teaspoons dried green herbs, such as thyme, basil, oregano, or a combination

Preheat the oven to 375°F. Wrap the tofu in a few layers of paper towel and set on a plate to drain some of the excess moisture.

To make the crust, combine the almond meal, salt, and rosemary in a bowl and stir to combine. Add the water and oil and stir until thoroughly combined. The dough should be wet and a bit crumbly.

Divide the dough equally among four 4-inch tart shell pans and use your fingers to gently press the dough evenly against the bottom and sides of the pans. Bake until the tarts look barely toasted and dry, 10 to 12 minutes. Remove and let cool on wire racks. Leave the oven on.

To make the filling, heat 1/2 tablespoon of the oil in a sauté pan over medium heat. Add the mushrooms and a pinch of salt. Continue to cook, stirring, until the mushrooms are browned and cooked through, 6 to 8 minutes. Transfer the mushrooms to a bowl and set aside. Add the remaining 1/2 tablespoon oil to the pan and add the onion. Cook until just caramelized, about 15 minutes.

It's not easy to find a gluten-free, dairy-free breakfast item that you'd serve to guests, even the kind of guests that *do* eat gluten and dairy, but these tarts would be perfect for brunch served with a simple side salad and some sliced fruit.

Silken tofu, which comes in an aseptic cardboard container at room temperature, is found at most regular grocery stores as well as health food stores. Though it is made of essentially the same thing as regular tofu, it's a bit smoother, and the two types are not interchangeable. Nutritional yeast is not exactly a pantry staple for most people, but vegans often have it on hand to add a somewhat cheesy flavor to foods. It is also full of some essential nutrients that vegans and vegetarians often miss out on. They sell it in bulk bins at health food stores, so you can buy as little as you want, but if you end up with more than you need here, it's great on roasted sweet potatoes or popcorn. Parmesan cheese would be a fine alternative. This recipe is written for individual tart pans, but if you increase the amount of each ingredient by 50 percent, it can be made in a standard pie pan, adding 10 minutes to the final cooking time.

In a food processor, combine the drained tofu, nutritional yeast, tahini, herbs, and 1/2 teaspoon salt and pulse a few times until smooth and combined (you could also do this with a potato masher in a bowl). Transfer to a mixing bowl. Once the onions and mushrooms are slightly cooled, stir them into the tofu mixture with a generous pinch of pepper. Let sit at room temperature for 10 minutes to allow the flavors to blend. The filling can be prepared a day in advance and kept covered in the fridge until ready to use.

Divide the filling among the tart shells. Put them back in the oven and bake until the tops are slightly browned, about 20 minutes. Remove and let cool.

Carefully remove the tarts from the shells (the crust is extremely delicate) and serve warm or at room temperature.

baby spinach frittata with sweet potato hash crust

SERVES 4 <

8 eggs

1/2 cup whole milk

Sea salt or smoked salt and freshly ground pepper

2 small sweet potatoes

1 tablespoon coconut oil or olive oil

1 teaspoon ground cumin

1 tablespoon fresh thyme leaves

2 green onions, white and green parts, thinly sliced

2 cups baby spinach

1/3 cup herbed fresh goat cheese (about 3 ounces)

Chopped fresh cilantro, for garnish

Hot sauce (optional)

Arrange a rack in the upper third of your oven and preheat the oven to 425°F.

In a large bowl, whisk the eggs together until uniform in color. Add the milk, a pinch of salt, and 1/2 teaspoon pepper, whisk, and set aside.

Peel the sweet potatoes and cut them into 1/4-inch cubes. Warm the oil in a 10- or 12-inch sauté pan over medium heat. Add the potatoes and toss to coat. Sprinkle the cumin, 1/2 teaspoon salt, and the thyme and stir again. Cook the sweet potatoes, tossing occasionally, until they are cooked through and have brown marks, about 10 minutes. Sprinkle the green onions on top of the potatoes, followed by the spinach. Let the spinach wilt, about 1 minute, putting a lid on the pan to help things along if you have one. Turn the heat down to low. Give the eggs one last whisk and pour them over the spinach. Break up the cheese with your fingers and distribute it over the top. Put the pan in the oven and bake until you can shake the pan and see that the middle is just barely set, 10 to 12 minutes. The handle will be very hot.

Put the frittata aside to set for a couple minutes before slicing it. Sprinkle with more pepper and garnish with the cilantro. Serve with hot sauce on the side.

Layers of flavor and only two dirty dishes—this is a dream breakfast. It's the perfect weekend dish to leave on the stove so you can take off little bites as the morning lingers. I learn things each time I make a frittata, which is often, as it's the perfect dish for using up leftover roasted vegetables or other produce. They are typically started on the stove and finished in the oven, which is less hassle than it sounds like as long as you keep an eye on the heat level. If you add the egg mixture to a scalding hot pan, you'll end up with burnt edges. Keep the burner on low when you pour in the eggs and gently warm everything up before putting it in the oven. It'll finish setting in the oven's heat and you won't end up with a burnt egg crust. The sweet potato hash protects the filling here, but it's worth noting anyway.

I recommend using a nonstick or cast-iron pan to ensure it comes out of the pan cleanly. The timing is based on a 10-inch pan. If you double the recipe, use something larger and adjust the cooking time as needed. If you want something heartier, such as for a holiday brunch, add some cooked chopped chicken sausage to the egg layer.

mango mint lassi

SERVES 2 <

¹/₄ cup freshly squeezed orange juice

1 large ripe mango, peeled and chopped

¹/₂ cup plain yogurt

1 cup crushed ice

1 tablespoon chopped fresh mint leaves

1 teaspoon honey, or more as needed

Combine all ingredients in a blender, starting with the juice on the bottom.

Blend well, until the blades are not catching on any solid pieces of mango or ice. Taste for sweetness and add more honey if you like. Divide between two glasses and drink immediately.

We spent our honeymoon in Indonesia, where I found the food to be a bit inconsistent, but I could always count on fresh lassis, which were served at all the restaurants, bars, hotels, and roadside stands. They are basically smoothies, but in Indonesia they aren't something you just drink in the morning.

I love the combination of mint and mango. The mint freshens up the creamy fruit mixture and totally hits the spot. If you want to make this more substantial, add in a bit of vanilla protein powder and a tad more orange juice. If you prefer it thinner, just add more orange juice as desired.

Salads and Sides

Some people may consider these recipes side dishes, but for me, these are the dishes that I eat most often. To me, the charm of salads and side dishes is the versatility they possess and how easily you can adapt them as you please. Once you learn how the different flavors and textures of foods play off of one another, you'll be able to work creatively with vegetables and suit them to whatever entrée you are serving.

Most days I am cooking for two, but a majority of these recipes are great to share with friends or make for great leftovers. We won't eat an entire pot of braised beans at dinner, but they're even better the next day. Whenever anyone writes to me for tips on eating healthier, I suggest that one of the easiest ways to help yourself is by having healthy choices available. Have salads and sides in the fridge that keep well, like the Honey Mustard Broccoli Salad (page 76), or snacks like the Beach Day Tuna Salad (page 142). If it's available when you need a nibble, you may reach for a few bites of it instead of the ice cream. I mean that in the humblest of ways as, let's be honest, I often reach for the ice cream instead of the broccoli; but it's always good to give yourself the option.

the house salad

1 large head butter or bibb lettuce

1 small jicama, peeled and cut into $^{1}/_{4}$-inch matchsticks (roughly $^{1}/_{2}$ cup)

$^{1}/_{3}$ cup pomegranate seeds

1 cup large shavings Asiago or Parmesan cheese

HOUSE DRESSING

2 $^{1}/_{2}$ tablespoons crème fraîche

2 tablespoons extra-virgin olive oil

1 teaspoon honey

1 scallion, white part only, finely chopped

2 tablespoons apple cider vinegar

$^{1}/_{2}$ teaspoon sea salt

$^{1}/_{2}$ teaspoon fresh ground pepper

To make the dressing, whisk together the crème fraîche, olive oil, and honey. Add the scallion, vinegar, salt, and pepper and whisk again. Taste and add salt and pepper to taste, or a touch more vinegar if you prefer your dressing on the acidic side.

Gently pull the lettuce leaves from the head, making sure they are dry. Gently toss the leaves and jicama with the dressing. Assemble in a stack on each of 4 plates, starting with the largest leaves on the bottom to create a base. Garnish each salad with a quarter of the pomegranate seeds and the cheese shavings. Serve immediately.

There is not much to say about this salad—it is as charmingly simple and straightforward as it appears. You could likely just copy it without a recipe. The point I do want to stress, however, is the necessity of making your own salad dressings. There is all sorts of junk in store-bought dressings and they don't taste nearly as fresh—not to mention that it's ridiculously easy to whisk a few things together or put them in a mini blender. This particular dressing hovers around the vinaigrette family, with just enough crème fraîche to coat the leaves with the thinnest amount of creaminess. Be sure your leaves are cleaned and fully dry so the dressing can cling on. The recipe yields enough for the given salads, but I typically double it so I have extra on hand.

grapefruit and crispy avocado salad

SERVES 6 <

2 pink grapefruits

1 cup brown rice crackers (about half of a 3.5-ounce package)

1 teaspoon sea salt

1 egg

2 firm but ripe avocados

4 cups mixed baby lettuces

$^1/_2$ cup thinly sliced radishes (optional)

2 tablespoons extra-virgin olive oil

2 tablespoons whole-milk Greek yogurt or sour cream

1 tablespoon agave nectar

Sea salt and freshly ground pepper

To segment the grapefruit, cut a slice off the bottom to create a flat surface. Place the grapefruit on the flat bottom and, using a chef's knife, cut from the top down following the curve of the fruit, removing all of the skin and the white pith. Working over a bowl to collect the juice, use a paring knife to slice along the membranes of the fruit, removing the small wedges between the membranes and reserving them in the bowl with their juices.

Preheat the oven to 450°F and line a baking sheet with parchment paper or foil.

Grind the rice crackers in a food processor until you get an even, sandlike texture. Transfer the cracker meal to a shallow bowl. Stir in the salt. In another shallow bowl, whisk the egg. Peel the avocados and cut into 1-inch wedges. Dredge an avocado slice in the egg, letting the extra drip off, then dredge it in the cracker meal. Place the slice on the baking sheet, curved ends up. Repeat with the remaining avocado slices and bake until toasty brown, 12 to 14 minutes. Remove from the oven and let cool.

In a large bowl, combine the lettuce, grapefruit segments (reserving their juice), and radishes.

Though this salad looks quite summery, the best-tasting citrus is actually available in the winter and early spring, when grapefruits have a sweetness to them instead of being strictly mouth-puckering. I've included how to segment the citrus so you don't get the bitter pith in your nice salad. It takes a bit of practice, but it's the best way I've found.

You can find brown rice crackers at most markets now, either near the crackers or in the Asian food section. Crisp brown rice cereal works well, too, if you can't find the crackers, though in this case you will need to add a bit more salt. If you're using the radishes, make sure they are sliced super thin so their strong flavor doesn't dominate the dish.

To make the dressing, add to the reserved (about ¼ cup) grapefruit juice the olive oil, yogurt, agave nectar, and a generous pinch of salt and pepper. Whisk to combine.

Add half of the dressing to the lettuce mixture and toss to combine. Taste and add more dressing to taste, if you like. Divide the dressed salad among 6 plates and top each serving with a few slices of the crispy avocado. Serve immediately.

haricot vert salad with avocado goddess dressing

SERVES 6 <

1 pound haricots verts, ends trimmed

1¹/₂ cups mixed baby tomatoes, halved

1 cup fresh corn kernels

¹/₂ cup cooked wheat berries (see page 231)

Sea salt and freshly ground pepper

DRESSING

¹/₃ cup buttermilk

Juice of ¹/₂ lemon

2 cloves garlic

¹/₄ cup loosely packed fresh flat-leaf parsley leaves, plus more for garnish

3 tablespoons chopped fresh chives, plus more for garnish

¹/₂ teaspoon sea salt

¹/₂ teaspoon freshly ground pepper

¹/₂ avocado, pitted and peeled

Prepare a large bowl of ice water and set aside. Bring a large pot of salted water to a boil. Blanch the haricots verts just long enough to take off the raw edge, 30 to 60 seconds. Using a slotted spoon, quickly transfer the haricots verts to the bowl of ice water for 1 minute to stop the cooking. Remove from the water, drain well, and pat dry.

While the beans are drying, prepare the dressing. In a blender or food processor, combine the buttermilk, lemon juice, garlic, parsley, chives, salt, and pepper and process until well combined. Add the avocado and pulse once or twice more to combine.

Toss the haricots verts, tomatoes, corn, and wheat berries with the desired amount of dressing. Sprinkle a bit of salt, pepper, and fresh chopped herbs on top and serve immediately.

I just love that word, "haricot vert," which refers to a thinner, more tender French green bean. A traditional American green bean is a fine alternative in this dish, but I would suggest cutting them in half on the diagonal (which makes them easier to eat) and also adding a minute to their blanching time. I like leaving the corn kernels raw for extra crunch, but they can stand a blanch with the green beans if you prefer a softer texture.

This dressing—a green goddess–type dressing that is thickened with fresh avocado instead of mayonnaise or sour cream—is one of my favorites. It doesn't save well, so this recipe makes pretty much exactly what you need to dress the vegetables.

One of my brilliant recipe testers suggested steel-cut oats as a gluten-free alternative to wheat berries. Simply soak them for a few hours, drain, and toss them in.

tuscan kale chopped salad

SERVES 4 <

PARMESAN VINAIGRETTE

1 small shallot, chopped

Juice of 1 Meyer lemon

1/4 cup freshly grated Parmesan cheese

1/3 cup extra-virgin olive oil

Sea salt and freshly ground pepper

2 slices rustic whole grain bread, torn into bite-size pieces

2 teaspoons extra-virgin olive oil

Pinch of sea salt

1 bunch lacinato (Tuscan) kale

1 apple, such as Braeburn, Gala, or Pink Lady

1 cup cooked chickpeas, chopped

1/2 cup toasted pecans, coarsely chopped

1/3 cup dried cherries, chopped

To make the vinaigrette, combine the shallot, lemon juice, Parmesan, and olive oil in a blender or food processor. Process until smooth, then add a pinch of salt and pepper and give one last pulse. Set aside.

Toss the bread with the olive oil and salt. Toast in a toaster oven or in a sauté pan over medium heat until the exterior of the bread is crispy, about 10 minutes.

To assemble the salad, cut the tough stems out of the kale and finely chop the leaves. Put the chopped kale in a large bowl. Core and dice the apple and add to the kale along with the chickpeas, pecans, and cherries. Add half of the dressing and toss to combine. Taste and add more dressing if you like. Divide among four salad plates and garnish each serving with the crispy croutons immediately before serving.

I love raw kale salads, in part because the nutrient-rich greens are so sturdy that the leftovers keep well. It's great if you pack your lunch for work or need something that will travel well to a picnic or potluck. For this recipe you'll want to use lacinato kale, which also goes by the name Tuscan kale. Its leaves are smoother and a bit more tender than those of curly kale, which is a bit uncomfortable to eat raw. If eating a salad made almost entirely of raw kale sounds daunting to you, substitute half of the kale with romaine lettuce to soften the texture and make the salad even more colorful.

This is a combination I think works well, but a variety of beans or dried fruit or nuts could be used depending on what you have on hand. The recipe here is simply to encourage you to try kale as a lettuce alternative. If I have one, I'll add a chopped hard-boiled egg or other leftover protein on top to fill me up. And be sure to chop everything into small, even pieces, as the beauty of a chopped salad is that you get a bit of everything in each bite.

papaya and red quinoa salad with mexican caesar dressing

SERVES 4 <

MEXICAN CAESAR DRESSING

Juice of $1/2$ Meyer lemon

1 tablespoon red wine vinegar

1 teaspoon honey

2 cloves garlic

$1/3$ cup finely grated Parmesan cheese

1 teaspoon ground ancho chile
powder

2 teaspoons Worcestershire sauce

Handful of fresh cilantro

$1/3$ cup extra-virgin olive oil

Sea salt

1 small papaya

1 large head romaine lettuce, chopped

$3/4$ cup cooked and cooled red quinoa
(see page 231)

$1/4$ cup thinly sliced red onion

$1/3$ cup roasted and salted pepitas
or roasted, salted, and chopped
macadamia nuts

To make the dressing, combine the lemon juice, vinegar, honey, garlic, Parmesan, chile powder, Worcestershire sauce, and cilantro in a blender or food processor and pulse to combine. Add the oil in a steady stream while continuing to pulse. Season to taste with salt.

Peel the papaya, scoop out the black seeds from the center, and cut the flesh into thin matchsticks. In a large mixing bowl, combine the romaine, quinoa, red onion, and pepitas and toss with a few spoonfuls of the dressing. Taste and add more dressing if you like. Gently toss once more with the papaya and serve immediately.

We typically take our family vacations with a few other families. It makes for fun memories to be in good company, share meals, entertain each other, and hang out by the beach or pool. A number of years ago we stayed at a house in Sayulita, Mexico, near Puerto Vallarta, where we had dinner brought in one night by a local restaurant. I can still remember the amazing salad they made with papaya and crisp greens. Even though it seemed a bit out of place with the rest of the food, I loved it, and I was glad it went unnoticed so I could take most of it for myself. I know there are people who don't think fruit has a place in savory foods, but I appreciate how it brightens things up. I took the vague memory of that salad in Sayulita and added to it a bit of quinoa for texture and protein and a Mexican Caesar dressing. Papayas, which are typically grown in tropical regions, are usually available year-round. You'll want one that is ripe but still fairly firm so that it will hold its shape as you peel it and doesn't get too mushy in the salad. For the dressing, if you can't find Meyer lemons, which are sweeter than regular lemons, add about another teaspoon of honey.

heirloom tomato stacks with bocconcini and kale pesto

SERVES 4 TO 6 <

KALE PESTO

1 small bunch lacinato (Tuscan) kale, stemmed and chopped (about 4 cups)

2 cloves garlic

1/3 cup freshly grated Parmesan cheese

Juice of 1 lemon

1/2 cup lightly toasted walnuts

2 tablespoons water

Sea salt and freshly ground pepper

1/4 to 1/3 cup extra-virgin olive oil

2 pounds assorted heirloom tomatoes (about 4 large tomatoes)

1 tablespoon extra-virgin olive oil

Flaked sea salt, such as Maldon

1 cup small mozzarella balls (baby bocconcini or pearline), drained

Freshly grated Parmesan cheese, for garnish

To make the pesto, bring a large pot of salted water to a boil. Cut the tough stems out of the kale and coarsely chop the leaves. Blanch the kale leaves until the color brightens, 30 seconds to 1 minute, then quickly transfer to a strainer and run cold water over them to stop the cooking. Once the kale is cool, squeeze out the excess water and set aside in the strainer. You should get about 1 1/2 cups of blanched kale.

In a food processor, combine the garlic, Parmesan, lemon juice, and walnuts and pulse to chop. Add the kale, water, and 1/2 teaspoon each of salt and pepper and pulse to combine. Turn the processor on and drizzle in the olive oil until you get the consistency you like. You will be tossing the mozzarella balls in the pesto, so it can't be too thick. Taste and adjust the salt and pepper, if necessary.

Slice the tomatoes and place the slices in a bowl. Drizzle the tablespoon of olive oil on top and sprinkle with a few pinches of salt flakes. In a separate bowl, toss the mozzarella with about 1/2 cup of the pesto.

Truth is, I don't care for raw tomatoes, but I once saw a Caprese salad stacked with such gorgeous heirloom tomatoes that I had to eat it just because it was so beautiful. Attractive food can change minds . . . well, my mind, at least.

We get our produce from a local CSA program, and the season for heavenly tomatoes is fairly short. It's longer than it is in most places, as we live in Southern California, but it's still a far cry from what mainstream supermarkets would lead you to believe by stocking tomatoes year-round. Between making tomato soup and this salad in the summer months, I make good use of that short season.

The kale pesto is a nutritionally dense take on a classic. It tastes slightly more earthy than its basil counterpart, but it is well matched with those sweet summer tomatoes and creamy balls of mozzarella. Any leftovers make a great sandwich spread or, with a bit more lemon juice added, a tasty salad dressing.

To assemble the dish, put a dollop of kale pesto on a salad plate and layer about three tomato slices on top of the pesto, with a few of the bocconcini between the slices. Repeat with the remaining ingredients. Sprinkle each plate with a bit of Parmesan and serve at room temperature.

toasted millet salad with arugula, quick pickled onions, and goat cheese

SERVES 6 <

QUICK PICKLED ONIONS

³/₄ cup apple cider or white vinegar

2 teaspoons sea salt

3 tablespoons natural cane sugar

1 dried bay leaf

4 whole cloves

1 red onion, thinly sliced

³/₄ cup millet

1¹/₃ cups low-sodium vegetable broth or water

2 teaspoons chopped fresh oregano leaves or ³/₄ teaspoon dried oregano

Sea salt

2 cups arugula

2 tablespoons extra-virgin olive oil

2 tablespoons white balsamic vinegar

¹/₃ cup toasted pine nuts

¹/₃ cup crumbled fresh goat cheese (about 3 ounces)

To make the quick pickled onions, in a saucepan, combine the vinegar, salt, sugar, bay leaf, and cloves and bring to a gentle boil over medium-high heat until the sugar is dissolved. Add the onion, stir, and remove the pan from the heat. Let the onions cool at room temperature, or transfer it all to a glass jar and put them in the fridge to speed the process along.

Put the millet in a heavy saucepan over medium-low heat. Cook, stirring frequently, until the millet is toasted, about 5 minutes. You will begin to smell a toasty aroma and they'll make a bit of a popping noise. Remove the pan from the heat and carefully add the broth (it will splatter a bit). Return to the heat and bring to a gentle simmer. Cover and cook for 15 minutes. Turn off the heat and let sit another 5 minutes before you remove the lid. Using a fork, break up the millet and fluff it, add the oregano and ¹/₂ teaspoon salt, stir, and set aside to cool completely.

I remember reading an article by Russ Parsons in the *LA Times* years back in which he sung the praise of grain salads as both nutritious and versatile. Whole grains each have their own special flavor, but they can also be used as a canvas for whatever other ingredients you want to throw in.

I prefer a lot of greens in my grain salads (which actually makes them more of a green salad with grain, but bear with me), and millet can go along with just about anything, it cooks quickly, is gluten-free, and is full of magnesium. I like to toast the millet before cooking, and I use slightly less water than you'd typically see suggested elsewhere, to make sure I get individual kernels as opposed to a pot of clumpy grain. The arugula and pickled onions have a kick to them, so they can stand up to the main dish of your choice, like some shrimp skewers or flank steak.

This recipe may yield more pickled onions than you'd like to use in your salad, although pickled onions are not as "oniony" as raw red onion, so don't be shy. Any leftovers will keep in the brine, in the fridge, for about a week. They're great for tacos or inside a packed veggie sandwich. The millet

Once the millet is cool, combine it with the arugula in a large bowl. Drizzle the olive oil and vinegar on top and gently toss to coat.

Drain the desired amount of pickled onion and add to the salad along with the pine nuts and goat cheese, giving it another toss. Taste and add more salt, if necessary, and serve.

and onions can be made in advance to save some time. Toss the millet in a bit of oil to keep it from drying out, and keep the onions in a covered glass jar or bowl in the fridge until ready to use.

golden beet salad with cider vinegar dressing

5 golden beets

1 tablespoon extra-virgin olive oil

$^3/_4$ cup apple cider vinegar

Sea salt

3 cups mâche or other tender greens

1 tablespoon walnut oil

Freshly ground pepper

$^1/_2$ cup toasted walnut pieces

$^1/_2$ cup ricotta salata or fresh goat cheese

Preheat the oven to 425°F.

Rinse the beets and cut off the greens, saving them for another use. Rub the beets with the olive oil, wrap in foil, and place on a baking sheet (in case they leak). Bake until you can pierce through the middle of each beet with a knife, about 1 hour. Remove from the oven and let cool.

While the beets are cooking, gently bring the vinegar to a boil in a small saucepan over medium heat until it is reduced by a third. Remove from the heat and let cool.

When the beets are cool, use a paring knife to remove the skins, which should peel off very easily. Cut each beet into thin slices using a sharp knife. Sprinkle them with salt and toss them in the reduced vinegar.

Toss the mâche with the walnut oil and a few grinds of pepper. Top the mâche with the beets, walnut pieces, and cheese. Use a spoon to drizzle the remaining vinegar on top, as desired. Serve immediately.

The contrast of colors

here makes this a beautiful salad for a dinner party or holiday meal. There are lovers and haters of beets, but I find the golden variety to be a bit milder than the red. It's a delicate salad with tender greens and thinly sliced beets that have an almost pickled flavor, their natural sweetness offset by the apple cider vinegar. The vinegar on the beets and the oil on the greens combine on the plate to make the salad's dressing. If you purchase a bunch of beets with the greens attached, save the greens; they are great chopped up in a salad and have a ton of nutritional value. You can prepare the beets up to a day in advance, toss them in vinegar, and store in the refrigerator in a covered container until you are ready to assemble the salad.

The warm nuttiness of walnut oil is a great complement to beets, but extra-virgin olive oil will work just fine too.

tangled carrot and broccoli sprout salad with tahini dressing

SERVES 4 <

1/3 cup French green (du Puy) lentils, rinsed

3/4 cup water

1 pound assorted orange, red, and purple carrots

2 1/2 cups broccoli sprouts

1/4 red onion, finely diced

1/2 cup toasted pistachios, coarsely chopped

TAHINI DRESSING

1/4 cup tahini

1 tablespoon extra-virgin olive oil

2 tablespoons agave nectar

3 tablespoons freshly squeezed lemon juice or apple cider vinegar

1/2 teaspoon sea salt

1/2 teaspoon freshly ground pepper

1 to 3 tablespoons water, as needed

Put the lentils in a pot with the water and bring to a gentle boil over medium-high heat. Reduce the heat to a simmer and cook, uncovered, until the lentils are tender, 15 to 20 minutes, adding water if the liquid has evaporated and the lentils are still tough. Drain the lentils and set aside to cool.

Using a vegetable peeler, peel the carrots. Rest the bottom of one of the peeled carrots on a cutting board. Starting at the skinny tip of the carrot, press firmly down the length of the carrot with the vegetable peeler to create thin shavings. Repeat with the remaining carrots. (If you prefer, you can use a mandoline instead.) Add the shaved carrots to a mixing bowl along with the broccoli sprouts and onion.

To make the dressing, in a separate small bowl, whisk together the tahini, olive oil, agave nectar, lemon juice, salt, and pepper. Add the water, 1 tablespoon at a time, until you reach the consistency of a basic vinaigrette.

Add the dressing to the bowl with the vegetables and toss to coat. Add the lentils and half of the pistachios and toss again. Sprinkle the remaining pistachios on top and serve immediately.

I have daydreams of owning a casual lunch spot with cases full of fresh, tasty salads and light entrées. Big white bowls would be filled with colorful seasonal salads that people could order to go or eat with a friend while enjoying a foamy cappuccino. There would be lots of exposed brick, plants, excellent coffee drinks, and servers who enjoyed being there, and we'd close on Sundays. I really can see every element of the Sprouted Kitchen Café in my mind—it's kind of ridiculous—but the first image that always comes to mind is the big bowls of salad. This colorful, crunchy dish, starring orange, red, and purple carrots, is something that would be served in that place. Getting out of the rut of thinking that salads must be made out of greens exclusively, this carrot-focused recipe makes an excellent side to sandwiches. You could make it an entrée by doubling the amount of lentils and adding some sturdy greens to fill it out. I have a sprout man at my farmers' market, and I know that some stores carry broccoli sprouts. If they are hard to come by where you are, you could use mâche, a very tender green, in its place. Try to find carrots that are on the larger side; they are easier to shave into strips.

stacked watermelon with feta and white balsamic

SERVES 4 <

1 small watermelon, chilled

1/2 cup feta cheese

1/3 cup white balsamic vinegar

3 tablespoons extra-virgin olive oil

Freshly ground pepper

4 cups baby arugula or watercress

2 cups fresh basil leaves, coarsely chopped

1/4 red onion, very thinly sliced

Cut the watermelon widthwise into 1/2-inch slices. Using a sharp round biscuit or cookie cutter, punch out circles from the flesh of the watermelon.

In a bowl, combine the feta, vinegar, olive oil, and a few grinds of pepper and stir together, smashing the feta with the back of a fork to break it up and create a rustic, somewhat chunky dressing.

Put the arugula, basil, and red onion in a bowl and toss with a few tablespoons of the dressing to coat. Put some of the greens on a plate and place a watermelon round on top. Drizzle a bit more dressing on the watermelon and continue stacking in the same way, alternating layers of greens, watermelon, and dressing, using all the ingredients to create stacks of equal size on four plates. Finish each serving with greens on top and serve immediately.

I'm a proponent of apples and Cheddar, pears and Stilton, berries and goat cheese . . . if it's sweet and salty, I'm into it. Though I am not the first to propose the combination presented here, I like to take the extra step of cutting the watermelon into rounds and stacking it with the contrasting greens, which makes a stunning salad. If you can get your hands on a yellow watermelon, alternate slices of red and yellow.

This would also make a nice appetizer if you simply piled some greens and dressing on top of one watermelon round, making them easy to eat with your hands.

fennel slaw

SERVES 4 <

2 large fennel bulbs, with a few
  chopped fronds

3 tablespoons extra-virgin olive oil

Grated zest of 1 Meyer lemon

3 tablespoons freshly squeezed Meyer
  lemon juice

2 or 3 tablespoons finely chopped
  fresh flat-leaf parsley

$1/2$ cup finely grated Parmesan cheese

Sea salt and freshly ground pepper

Using a mandoline or a sharp chef's knife, slice the fennel bulbs
horizontally as thinly as you can. Remove any large core parts, then
add the slices to a large mixing bowl with the fronds.

Add the olive oil and lemon zest and juice to the bowl and toss with
your hands. Let it sit for about ten minutes to soften the fennel. You
could do this up to two days in advance.

Before serving, add the parsley, Parmesan, a pinch or two of salt, and
a generous grind of black pepper. Toss everything together and serve
immediately.

At many bars in Italy, they have what is called an *aperitivo*, when you can enjoy a buffet of appetizers with the purchase of a drink. Sometimes the food is so tasty you could easily make a dinner of it, as I usually did when I was there as a college student. I can still visualize the unassuming alley where my friend and I found a bar serving a fresh and perfectly salty fennel slaw. I remember eating plates full of it and jotting down what was in it so I could replicate it myself. The nutty Parmesan and zesty lemon in this dish are unapologetic, making this salad bold and flavorful. If you do some of the prep work in advance, save the addition of cheese and salt until the last minute, since the salt will begin to pull the water from the fennel, reducing the vegetable's fresh crunch. Still, I appreciate how well this salad keeps in the fridge. It definitely softens, but almost to its benefit, like a marinade, not getting too soggy before you can polish off the bowl. If the texture or flavor is too much for you, add a bit of lettuce to the bowl to break it up—the recipe yields enough dressing to coat it as well.

braised white beans and leeks

SERVES 6 TO 8 <

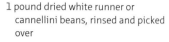

1 pound dried white runner or
   cannellini beans, rinsed and picked
   over

3 large leeks

1 tablespoon extra-virgin olive oil

2 celery stalks, diced

4 cloves garlic, coarsely chopped

2 tablespoons fresh thyme leaves

2 teaspoons herbes de Provence

1/2 to 1 teaspoon red pepper flakes

Sea salt and freshly ground black
   pepper

4 cups low-sodium vegetable broth

1 cup shredded mozzarella

1/2 cup freshly grated Parmesan
   cheese

Soak the beans, uncovered, in a large bowl of cold water on the counter for at least 4 hours, or up to overnight. Drain and set aside.

Arrange a rack in the lower third of your oven and preheat the oven to 225°F.

Trim the leeks, discarding the tough green tops, halve vertically, and rinse in cold water, making sure to clean out any dirt trapped between the layers. Slice into thin half circles. In a large Dutch oven or ovenproof casserole over medium heat, warm the olive oil. Add the celery, garlic, and leeks and cook until the vegetables are softened, 3 to 5 minutes.

Add the beans, thyme, herbes de Provence, red pepper flakes to taste, 3/4 teaspoon salt, and a generous amount of black pepper. Stir in the vegetable broth and 1/2 cup water and bring the mixture back up to a gentle boil. Cover the pot with an ovenproof lid or cover it tightly with foil. Place in the oven and cook, checking occasionally to make sure the pot is never dry, until the beans are soft throughout but not falling apart, 3 to 3 1/2 hours. If the pot seems dry, add water in 1/2-cup increments and stir once or twice. Taste and adjust the salt and pepper if necessary.

I once worked at a bed-and-breakfast in Italy where Lucy, the lovely woman I worked for, had mastered the art of simple dishes. Guests raved about a side dish she made that was basically sautéed leeks and canned white butter beans dressed with her own olive oil. I can still hear her adorably obvious response, which Hugh and I frequently (and lovingly) mimic, "It's just leeks and beans!" I have complicated her recipe a bit, but this pot of braised beans is my ultimate side dish.

This pot of beans proves that a healthy side can indeed be decadent. Cooking with fresh, high-quality beans has made a complete believer of me. My favorite source is Northern California distributor Rancho Gordo, which produces heirloom beans so fresh that they cook more quickly than others. As happens when cooking something low and slow, the beans become creamy and the leeks permeate the whole pot with their humble onion sweetness. The cheese, added in the last moments of cooking, completes the dish in my opinion, but some toasted

Remove the pot from the oven and turn the oven heat up to 500°F. Sprinkle the mozzarella and Parmesan on top of the bean mixture and put the pot back in the oven, leaving the lid off. Cook until the cheese is completely melted and brown in spots, 8 to 10 minutes. Serve hot.

bread crumbs with a drizzle of good extra-virgin olive oil would be great as well. You could also stir in a scant cup of crispy cooked, crumbled bacon just before you put the cheese on top. If you go this route, you probably need less salt.

honey mustard broccoli salad

SERVES 4 TO 6 <

2 bunches broccoli with stems (about 1 pound total)

$1/2$ cup toasted sunflower seeds

1 apple, such as Gala, Fuji, or Honeycrisp, cored and diced

$1/4$ cup finely chopped fresh flat-leaf parsley

HONEY DIJON DRESSING

3 tablespoons Dijon mustard

2 tablespoons honey

2 tablespoons extra-virgin olive oil

2 tablespoons red wine vinegar

Pink salt and freshly ground pepper

Cut the stems from the broccoli and set aside. Cut the florets into bite-size pieces. In a large pot with a steamer insert, steam the florets just long enough to take off the raw edge, about 1 minute. Drain and let cool. While the broccoli cools, julienne the stems using a julienne peeler or a mandoline.

To make the dressing, in a large mixing bowl, whisk together the mustard, honey, olive oil, and vinegar with a pinch or two of salt and a generous amount of freshly ground pepper. Add the broccoli florets, broccoli stems, sunflower seeds, apple, and parsley to the bowl and toss to coat.

Chill in the fridge for at least 30 minutes. Serve cold.

Near our place is this wonderful picnic spot that sits above the Pacific Ocean. It's the place I go if I need to think, write, celebrate a birthday, or even go on a romantic date. Sometimes I pick up food along the way, but I also like to pack a few things that travel well. This broccoli salad is the perfect side for a picnic. The broccoli florets are just barely steamed to take the raw edge off, the stems get julienned for more texture, and the apples and seeds give it just enough crunch. If you don't have a tool to julienne the stems, well-stocked markets sell broccoli slaw, which is the stems already shredded for you. Thinly sliced green cabbage would be a nice alternative as well.

delicata squash sformato

SERVES 4 <

1 large delicata squash (about 3 pounds)

1/2 cup crème fraîche, at room temperature

1/2 cup shredded Jack cheese

2 teaspoons fresh thyme leaves

1/2 teaspoon sea salt

1/2 teaspoon freshly ground pepper

2 tablespoons maple syrup

1 tablespoon balsamic vinegar

1 egg, beaten

1/2 teaspoon freshly grated nutmeg

Preheat the oven to 400°F.

Cut the squash in half lengthwise, remove the seeds, and pierce a few holes in the skin. Place the squash cut side down in a glass baking dish and roast in the oven until soft, 40 to 45 minutes. The timing may vary, so keep an eye on it. You want a few brown blisters and to be able to pierce it easily with a fork. Set aside and let cool.

Put the crème fraîche, Jack cheese, thyme, salt, and pepper in a bowl and stir to combine.

Once the squash is cool enough to handle, scoop the flesh away from the skin and put it in a bowl. Add the maple syrup and balsamic vinegar and mash the squash until smooth. Add the cheese mixture and stir to combine. Add the egg and nutmeg, giving the mixture a final stir.

Grease an 8 by 8-inch baking dish on all sides and pour in the squash mixture. Turn the oven down to 375°F and bake until brown spots start to show on top, 30 to 40 minutes. Allow it to rest for 10 minutes before serving.

A *sformato* is essentially a soufflé that doesn't rise because there isn't any air or egg white whipped into it—foolproof! I serve it in place of mashed potatoes, since it has a great flavor without an excess of butter and cream. If I have people over, I'll bake it in individual gratin dishes with a few fresh thyme leaves on top for presentation's sake.

Delicata squash has a flavor similar to that of butternut, but the skin is much thinner—edible, in most cases—and the squash is more delicate overall (hence the name). The flesh of a butternut or acorn squash would be a fine substitute. Cooking with squash in the fall and early winter months will yield the best results with this recipe. I find that out of season the squash become a bit waterlogged. You can do everything but bake the *sformato* in advance. Bring the dish to room temperature before baking.

brussel leaf and
baby spinach sauté

SERVES 4 <

1 pound brussels sprouts

2 tablespoons extra-virgin olive oil

1 tablespoon white wine or
champagne vinegar

1 tablespoon maple syrup

4 cups baby spinach

2 generous pinches of sea salt

$1/2$ cup Marcona almonds

Working with one brussels sprout at a time, peel each individual leaf, starting from the outside and working toward the middle. Continue to peel until you get to the tough core where it is just too tight to pull any more leaves. Discard the core and put the leaves in a big bowl. Repeat with the remaining brussels sprouts.

Over medium heat, warm the olive oil in a large frying pan. Add all of the brussels leaves and sauté for about 30 seconds. Add the vinegar and maple syrup and toss to coat. Add the spinach to the pan and toss until it is just barely wilted. It is better just slightly underdone in this case, as it will continue to cook in its own heat.

Sprinkle with the salt and Marcona almonds and serve immediately.

If you are the cook around the house, you know how sweet the words "I love this. Please make it again!" sound. This side has become my go-to dish for something quick and pretty, as I love the juxtaposition of the two shades of green. After you remove the leaves from the brussels sprouts, this takes only minutes to prepare. Brussels sprouts are miniature balls of cabbage, so their stems can be pretty tough. By working from the outermost leaf inward, and cutting more of the stem whenever necessary, you follow the pattern of the sprout to easily remove its leaves. You can do this part in advance, but you'll want to sauté them just before serving.

Marcona almonds are blanched Spanish almonds that are sweeter than American almonds. They can run on the expensive side, but I have seen them at both Trader Joe's and Costco for a reasonable price. You don't need a lot of them, but their flavor is really special on top of this plate of tender greens.

young carrots en papillote

SERVES 4 <

1¹/₄ pounds small (about 4-inch) carrots, scrubbed and tops removed

Generous drizzle of olive oil or melted unsalted butter

1 small handful fresh thyme, savory, tarragon, or a combination

Flaked sea salt, such as Maldon, and freshly ground pepper

¹/₂ cup white wine

Preheat the oven to 425°F.

Lay out a piece of parchment paper or foil about 2 feet long. Place the carrots in the center and drizzle them generously with the olive oil, or the melted butter, if you prefer. Add the herbs (it should look like a lot of herbs, so load them up) and a few pinches of both salt and pepper and give the carrots a quick toss. Fold up the edges of the parchment and pour the wine on top. Fold the parchment over to make a pouch and scrunch the edges together to lightly seal.

Bake until the carrots are just tender, 30 to 35 minutes. Carefully unwrap the packet, so as not to burn yourself as the steam escapes, and spoon any sauce on the bottom of the packet on top of the carrots. Serve warm.

I am a bit of a roasting addict when it comes to fall and winter vegetables, but carrots come out so tender when cooked with a bit of steam. Cooking *en papillote* is a French term for cooking something in a parchment pouch (though you can use foil as well). The pouch holds in the moisture, whether it is stock, water, or wine, and gently steams the food. The cleanup is easy, and the cooking method doesn't distract from the sweet, tender carrots.

I go between using olive oil and butter in this recipe, depending on who I am making these for and what I am serving them with. The butter results in more of a sauce and a bit more creaminess, while the olive oil leaves the carrots tasting slightly lighter.

winter wild rice casserole

SERVES 4 TO 6 <

1 bunch Swiss chard

1 egg

3 cloves garlic, minced

1 cup ricotta

1/2 cup grated Gruyère

2 cups cooked wild rice (see page 231)

1 cup cooked brown rice
(see page 231)

1 tablespoon red wine vinegar

1 teaspoon sea salt

1 teaspoon freshly ground pepper

6 sun-dried tomatoes in oil

1 tablespoon extra-virgin olive oil

Chopped fresh basil, for garnish

Preheat the oven to 400°F.

Remove the thick stems from the Swiss chard and coarsely chop the leaves. Prepare a bowl of ice water. Bring a large pot of salted water to a boil and blanch the chard for about 1 minute. Immediately transfer the chard to the ice water so that it stops cooking and retains its color. Set it in a strainer and press out the water.

In a large bowl, whisk the egg until uniform in color and doubled in volume. Add the garlic to the bowl. Add the ricotta, Gruyère, wild rice, brown rice, vinegar, and salt and pepper and stir to combine. Break up the clumps of chard with your fingers and add it to the bowl with the rice mixture. Chop the sun-dried tomatoes into small pieces and add them to the bowl along with any oil that has collected on the cutting board. Stir until everything is combined.

Grease an 8 by 8-inch baking dish and pour in the rice mixture. Drizzle the olive oil on top and bake in the oven until it is set but the center is still a bit soft, about 20 minutes. The center will continue to set as it sits.

Once the casserole has cooled slightly, sprinkle it with the chopped basil and serve warm.

We tried to photograph

this tasty dish, but its casserole-esque texture and mélange of colors mislead you as to how it tastes. The aesthetic just doesn't communicate the toothsome texture of the rice, sweet richness of the sun-dried tomatoes, and just enough creamy cheese to bind it all together. This dark casserole is the perfect dish for a cold night. And, since it travels well and can be eaten as is or alongside a main dish, it is the perfect dish to bring friends who are sick or just had a baby.

You can experiment with cheeses besides Gruyère, or use any sort of leafy green vegetable in place of the Swiss chard. See the chart on page 231 for information on cooking the rice. You can make the rice a day in advance, coat the grains with a dash of oil, and keep it in the fridge until you are ready to assemble the dish. The rice takes time, not attention, so you can carry on with other things while it cooks.

mashies and greens

SERVES 6 <

3 pounds potatoes, such as Yukon gold

1 bunch lacinato (Tuscan) kale

1/3 cup plus 1 teaspoon olive oil, or more as needed

3 cloves garlic, minced

1 1/2 cups buttermilk or whole milk, at room temperature

1 tablespoon prepared horseradish (optional)

1/2 to 3/4 cup freshly grated Parmesan or Grana Padano cheese, at room temperature

1 teaspoon sea salt

Freshly ground pepper

Cut the potatoes in half. Put them in a large pot and cover completely with tepid water. Add a few pinches of salt and bring the water to a boil. Cook until the potatoes are tender, 20 to 25 minutes.

While the potatoes cook, stem the kale and chop the leaves. Heat 1 teaspoon of the olive oil in a small sauté pan over medium-low heat and sauté the garlic until softened, 1 to 2 minutes.

When the potatoes are tender, drain them and return to the pot. Add the kale, garlic, the remaining 1/3 cup of olive oil, and 3/4 cup of the buttermilk and mash together. Add the horseradish and 1/2 cup of the Parmesan and mash again. Add the remaining 3/4 cup of buttermilk until you get the consistency you like, remembering that they will continue to absorb moisture as they sit. Stir in 1 teaspoon of salt and pepper to taste and more olive oil if they need more moisture. Serve with the remaining Parmesan sprinkled on top.

I made up this dish for my beloved sister, who could survive off carbohydrates alone. She has always called mashed potatoes "mashies," her term of endearment for the side dish that takes up the majority of her holiday dinner plate.

This recipe represents the yin and yang of how I like to cook, pairing vibrant kale, which has tons of nutrition, with the tasty comfort of a bowl of warm potatoes. There are vitamins A, D, E, and K and lots of potassium in this dish, while there is also oil, cheese, and salt—and that is all great with me.

I leave the skin on the potatoes here for even more fiber and the rustic look it gives the dish. You are welcome to peel the potatoes, or run them through a food mill if you prefer a finer, more consistent texture. Seek out Yukon gold or Yellow Finn potatoes, which are moister than russet potatoes, so you don't have to use an excessive amount of fat to keep them from being dry. The buttermilk makes a more tart dish, while the whole milk makes it more neutral. Take your pick.

roasted acorn squash with hazelnuts and balsamic reduction

SERVES 4 TO 6 <

2 medium acorn squash

6 cloves garlic, unpeeled

3 tablespoons hazelnut or olive oil

1 teaspoon sea salt

Freshly ground pepper

1 cup balsamic vinegar

³/₄ cup crème fraîche

1 tablespoon finely chopped fresh oregano

¹/₄ cup toasted hazelnuts, skins removed and coarsely chopped

Preheat the oven to 400°F.

Cut the ends from the squash, cut in half lengthwise, and scoop out the seeds. Slice each half into four wedges. Spread all of the squash pieces and the garlic cloves on a rimmed baking sheet. Drizzle on the hazelnut oil and sprinkle with the salt and 1 teaspoon pepper. Toss with your hands, rubbing each piece of squash to be sure it is coated with oil. If you like to be more intentional, you can use a brush to paint the oil on each acorn wedge. Bake in the oven until browned on the edges and cooked through, about 25 minutes.

While the squash are baking, put the balsamic vinegar in a small saucepan over medium heat and let it gently boil until reduced by half, 8 to 10 minutes. Remove from the heat. It will also thicken as it cools, so watch it carefully; if you let it boil too long, it will be impossible to pour.

Put the crème fraîche in a small bowl and add a few grinds of fresh pepper. When the roasted vegetables are just cool enough to touch, push the garlic out of their skins into the crème fraîche. Use the back of a fork to smash the garlic, blending it into the cream.

When it comes to holiday meals, I love the sentiment, the crazy family dynamics, and even the big mess that ends with everyone washing dishes and drying wine glasses. But the traditional food? Not so much. I have Filipino in-laws, who make a stuffed turkey with mint jelly, hard-boiled eggs, olives, and whatnot, so the competition to bring something unique is really fierce. If, however, you are having a more traditional feast, with its bounty of heavy dishes, it is just asking for a side like this. Sure, there is a decadence to the roasted garlic crème fraîche, but the small dab of creaminess is simply an accent and doesn't take over the entire dish. This dish is sweet, creamy, crunchy, and savory all at once, reminding me to eat slowly and appreciate how the ingredients complement each other.

I have tried this with both acorn and kabocha squash, and both work fabulously, but acorn squash have a bit nicer texture and are easier to find. You will lose a finger if you try to cut through winter squash with a dull knife, so sharpen your knives before you go at this bulky vegetable.

To serve individually, place a few wedges of squash on a plate, drizzle with the balsamic glaze, sprinkle with the oregano and hazelnuts, and place a dollop of crème fraîche in the middle. When assembling a larger platter, serve the crème fraîche on the side.

roasted asparagus with bread crumbs and herbs

SERVES 6 <

1 3/4 cups coarsely chopped bread crumbs, made from day-old bread

1 tablespoon Dijon mustard

1 teaspoon whole grain mustard

2 teaspoons fresh thyme leaves or 1 teaspoon dried thyme

2 1/2 tablespoons extra-virgin olive oil

Sea salt and freshly ground pepper

Grated zest of 2 lemons

1/4 cup fresh flat-leaf parsley, finely chopped

1/2 cup freshly grated Parmesan cheese

3 hard-boiled eggs

2 1/2 pounds asparagus, trimmed

1 garlic clove, minced

2 teaspoons lemon pepper

Arrange a rack in the upper third of your oven and preheat the oven to 400°F.

In a bowl, stir together the bread crumbs, mustards, thyme, 1 1/2 table-spoons of the olive oil, and a big pinch of salt and pepper. Spread on a rimmed baking sheet and bake until toasted, 10 to 12 minutes. Transfer to a mixing bowl and let cool completely.

When the bread crumbs are cool, add the lemon zest, parsley, and Parmesan. Dice the eggs and add to the bread crumb mixture.

Turn the oven up to 425°F. On a baking sheet, toss the asparagus with the remaining 1 tablespoon olive oil, the garlic, and the lemon pepper, adding another generous pinch of salt if your lemon pepper doesn't contain salt. Roast in the oven until the asparagus just starts to blister, about 10 minutes, though the time may vary depending on the thickness of the stalks.

Transfer the asparagus to a serving platter and spoon the bread crumb mixture across the center. Serve warm.

My favorite thing about this dish is that it can stand on its own as the single side dish. The tender asparagus, salty cheese, crisp crumbs, and protein-filled eggs—it hits every point. The game changer for this recipe is how you make the bread crumbs. If you have an end of a baguette or any fresh bread that has dried out, break it into a few pieces and pulse it in the food processor until you get very coarse crumbs. This does take some forethought, so if I ever find myself with stale bread, I do this and keep the bread crumbs in the freezer so I always have them on hand. The boxed bread crumbs available at the market are too powdery to give this dish the right crunch. Panko, or Japanese bread crumbs, have some texture to them and could work as a last resort.

Though I think this dish is perfect for a party, I don't recommend prepar-ing it in advance. The bread crumbs will be nice and crisp when they are freshly toasted, but if they sit they will become soft and chewy. I use aspara-gus spears of medium width here; this isn't really the place for the super-thin or jumbo kind.

To hard-boil eggs without a gray ring around the yolk, put the eggs in a pot and fill with just enough cool water to cover them. Bring the water to a boil, let the eggs boil gently for about 3 minutes, and then turn off the heat. Set a timer for 18 minutes. When the timer dings, drain the eggs and transfer to a bowl of ice water for at least 5 minutes. Be sure the water stays cold, as this will make the shell easy to remove.

spiced sweet potato wedges

SERVES 6 <

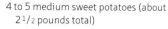

4 to 5 medium sweet potatoes (about 2¹/₂ pounds total)

2 tablespoons extra-virgin olive oil or coconut oil

2 teaspoons smoked paprika

1 teaspoon garlic powder

Pinch of chipotle chile powder (optional)

3 tablespoons chopped fresh rosemary

Sea salt and freshly ground pepper

DIP

1¹/₂ avocados

¹/₂ cup buttermilk

2 tablespoons freshly squeezed lemon juice

2 cloves garlic, minced

Few pinches of chopped fresh flat-leaf parsley

Few pinches of chopped fresh chives

Sea salt and freshly ground pepper

Arrange a rack in the upper third of your oven and preheat the oven to 425°F.

Scrub the sweet potatoes, pat dry, and cut them into 8 wedges each. On a rimmed baking sheet, toss the wedges with the olive oil. Sprinkle with the paprika, garlic powder, chile powder, rosemary, and a generous amount of salt and pepper and toss again to coat. Spread them out in an even layer with as little overlap as possible.

Roast in the oven, flipping the wedges over and rotating the pan halfway through, until the outside of the wedges are crisp, 30 to 35 minutes. There should be dark spots on the wedges; don't worry.

While the potatoes roast, make your dip. Peel and pit both of the avocados. Dice the ¹/₂ avocado and set aside. In a bowl, combine the flesh of the whole avocado, the buttermilk, lemon juice, garlic, parsley, chives, and few pinches of salt and pepper. Use a whisk to combine well or transfer to a blender and pulse until combined. Stir in the chopped avocado to give it a chunky texture.

Sprinkle the potato wedges with a few more pinches of salt and serve with the dipping sauce on the side.

There are few starches I like more than sweet potato wedges with a crispy crust and a sweet, soft center. I tried many times to make sweet potato "fries" by baking them instead of frying them, but, because of the vegetable's water content, they always came out on the floppy side, never quite like the classic deep-fried version, a cooking method I was not willing to do at home. The secret is to embrace that water content. By roasting wedges in high heat with a light coat of oil, it guarantees that the outside will get crisp, while they're in there for just enough time to fully cook through inside. Choose sweet potatoes with orange flesh that are similar in size for even cooking time.

The dip is almost the same as the dressing used on the Haricot Vert Salad (page 56), but it's made a little thicker with some chunks of avocado. They would also be great with a home-made ranch or a mild blue cheese dressing.

Mains

Included in this chapter is a full gamut of main courses, including both veg-etarian meals and a few seafood and poultry dishes. Although I am a die-hard snacker myself and could live on the sides, salads, and other nibbles in this book, I also enjoy sharing meals and feeding other people, so I make these dishes when I'm cooking for family and friends. Sometimes it's not just the food itself but the memories related to it that ties us to certain recipes. I have some sweet memories about making many of these dishes, which I served at a few dinner parties with friends so that I could get some feedback on what I was working on. I really enjoy watching the people I love get together in the name of a good meal, and I'm so lucky that my work and pleasure overlap.

It's important to me that I make something that's both nutritious and tastes good, and when I make vegetarian meals, I try to make something that's hearty and tasty enough even for people who also eat meat—I lure them over with Asian Tofu Tacos with Hoisin Slaw or Beer Bean– and Cotija-Stuffed Poblanos. Whether you're looking for inspiration for a weeknight din-ner or a backyard barbecue, you'll find something here to suit every occasion and inclination.

asian tofu tacos with hoisin slaw

SERVES 4 <

1 (14-ounce) package extra-firm tofu

³/₄ teaspoon Chinese five-spice powder

3 tablespoons rice vinegar

2 cloves garlic, minced

2-inch piece of fresh ginger, peeled and grated

1¹/₂ tablespoons toasted sesame oil

Pinch of sea salt

1 Asian pear

¹/₂ cup hoisin sauce

¹/₃ cup low-fat plain yogurt

5 green onions, white and light green parts, chopped

2¹/₂ cups finely shredded green or napa cabbage

8 small whole grain or brown rice tortillas

Cut the tofu into 1-inch cubes and set on a plate lined with a few paper towels. Set aside to drain for at least 15 minutes, up to a few hours in the fridge.

In a bowl, stir together the five-spice powder, 2 tablespoons of the rice vinegar, the garlic, ginger, 1 tablespoon of the sesame oil, and salt. Pat the tofu dry. In a shallow dish, gently toss the tofu in the spice mixture. Let it marinate at room temperature for 15 minutes to 1 hour.

While the tofu marinates, core the pear and thinly slice. In a large bowl, whisk together the hoisin sauce, yogurt, and the remaining 1 tablespoon of vinegar. Set aside.

Heat the remaining ¹/₂ tablespoon of oil in a large frying pan over medium-high heat. Add ³/₄ of the green onions (setting the rest aside for garnish) and the tofu mixture and all its marinade into the pan. Sauté until the edges of the tofu are browned, 8 to 10 minutes.

Toss the cabbage in the hoisin mixture to coat. Heat the tortillas over the stove flame. To assemble the tacos, fill each of the tortillas with some of the dressed cabbage, a few slices of pear, and some of the tofu mixture. Garnish with the remaining green onions and serve.

I got this idea from a food truck in Los Angeles. Like most people, I think of Mexican flavors when I think of tacos, so I was grateful for the inspiration to try something different. At the food truck, they double-fry their tofu, which I couldn't bring myself to do, but there is plenty of crunch going on in this dish, so you won't miss the deep-frying.

I find most hoisin sauce to be a bit too sweet, but here the yogurt mellows it out. If you want to make a vegan version of this dish, try using Tofutti sour cream instead of the yogurt or even just mixing the hoisin with a bit of rice vinegar to balance out that sweetness. You'll want the cabbage pretty well dressed, as it adds a lot of dimension to the dish. If using a tortilla with Asian ingredients is a little too strange for you, put the fillings in some lettuce leaves and make lettuce wraps instead.

beer bean– and
cotija-stuffed poblanos

SERVES 6 <

BEER BEANS

$^1/_2$ pound dried pinto or Rio Zape
    beans, rinsed and picked over

1 teaspoon extra-virgin olive oil

1 yellow onion, halved and sliced

2 cloves garlic, minced

12 ounces dark Mexican beer, such as
    Negra Modelo

$^1/_2$ teaspoon chipotle chile powder,
    or 1 canned chipotle chile in adobo,
    chopped

$^1/_2$ teaspoon ground cinnamon

Sea salt

6 poblano chiles

1 cup crumbled cotija cheese

1 cup shredded Jack cheese

Juice of $^1/_2$ lime

1 tablespoon extra-virgin olive oil

$^1/_2$ cup chopped fresh cilantro

Place the beans in a large glass bowl and cover them generously with water. Allow them to soak for at least 6 hours, or up to overnight.

Drain the beans of their soaking liquid. In a large pot over medium heat, add the olive oil, onion, and garlic and sauté until the onion is just softened. Add the soaked beans and 2$^1/_2$ cups water, give them a stir, and bring the beans to a simmer. Simmer until the beans are cooked through, 45 minutes to 1 hour. Add the beer, chipotle, and cinnamon and simmer until most of the liquid is absorbed and the beans are tender, about another 20 minutes, depending on the freshness of the beans. If necessary, add a bit of water as the beans cook to keep the pot from drying out. Add $^1/_2$ to $^3/_4$ teaspoon of salt, to taste, and cook another 10 minutes. Set the beans aside.

Cut a slit down the side of each poblano. Remove and discard the membranes and seeds from inside the chile and set the chile on a baking sheet. Repeat with the remaining poblanos. Preheat the grill to medium-high heat, leaving one section over indirect heat. In a bowl, mix the cotija and Jack cheeses with the lime juice. Stuff each pepper with a few spoonfuls of the beans and a handful of the cheese

I do love a good chile relleno, but they typically run a bit heavy on the cheese. In this recipe, however, the chiles are also stuffed with beans that have a lot of flavor, and because they add a bit of protein, this makes a great vegetarian entrée. This is undoubtedly one of my favorite recipes, and I serve it to meat eaters without hesitation, as I know it has enough substance and flavor to hold its own. I make them on an outdoor grill or on the stove with a grill pan, but they can also be roasted in the oven for the same amount of time if that's easier for you. Making the beans from scratch takes some planning ahead, but in a pinch, you can use about 2 cups of canned pinto beans. Rinse and drain the beans and then follow the directions with the onions and seasonings, using just the beer (but no water) to simmer it all, uncovered, for about 10 to 15 minutes, and go from there.

Serve these with some Spanish rice and a simple green salad to make them a meal, but they also work great as a side dish as part of a larger Mexican-themed spread.

mixture. Brush the outside of each poblano with the olive oil and grill the peppers over direct heat, rotating them every few minutes to evenly char the outsides, 6 to 8 minutes total. Move them to indirect heat for another 8 to 10 minutes, until the insides are melty and the peppers have softened a bit. Serve the peppers immediately with the slit side up and garnished with the cilantro.

roasted tomato soup

SERVES 4 <

2 pounds ripe tomatoes

1 small yellow onion

1 tablespoon extra-virgin olive oil

Sea salt and freshly ground pepper

2 tablespoons chopped fresh flat-leaf
  parsley

3 cloves garlic

1 1/2 cups low-sodium vegetable broth

2 tablespoons tomato paste

1/2 cup heavy cream or whole milk

4 slices thick, whole grain bread

4 slices mozzarella

Fresh oregano or basil leaves, for
  garnish

Preheat the oven to 350°F.

Cut the tomatoes and onion into wedges. Use your fingers to scoop out some of the biggest pockets of seeds. Spread the tomatoes and onion on a rimmed baking sheet. Drizzle with the olive oil and sprinkle with 1/2 teaspoon salt, a generous amount of pepper, and the parsley. Gently toss with your hands to combine. Tuck the garlic cloves in the nook of a tomato so they won't burn in the oven. Roast until the tomatoes have broken down and reduced to about half their original size, 30 to 40 minutes. Remove from the oven and let cool slightly.

In a large pot over medium heat, warm the broth and stir in the tomato paste to dissolve. Add all of the ingredients from the baking sheet to the broth and simmer gently for 5 minutes. Using an immersion blender, food processor, or blender, puree the soup until it is smooth but still has some texture. If you prefer a silkier soup, pass it through a fine-mesh sieve. Return the soup to the pot, turn the heat to low, and stir in the cream. Add more salt and pepper to taste.

If you're serving the soup with cheesy toast, drizzle each slice of bread with a bit of olive oil and a slice of the mozzarella. Toast them in a toaster oven or under a broiler until the cheese is melted, about 5 minutes. Float a toast in each bowl of soup. Garnish with the oregano and serve hot.

Simple things are usually the best. You can spend hours on an involved recipe, running around to different markets getting unique ingredients, but sometimes it's the things we make with what's in the fridge that taste perfect.

This soup is the result of a summer when our CSA box was brimming full of tomatoes in a household that doesn't care for raw tomatoes. Roasting them reduces the water content, so you are left with a rich, almost smoky flavor. Made only with familiar ingredients and as straightforward as it gets, this soup is ideal for the surplus of tomatoes at the end of summer. We turn this into a meal by floating "cheesy toast" in the soup, but serving it with a classic grilled cheese sandwich would be perfect too. Otherwise, I sometimes throw in a few turkey meatballs for those who want the extra protein.

This soup could easily be made dairy-free by using soy or almond milk instead of the cream, though the result will be slightly thinner.

smoky red lentil soup

SERVES 4 <

2 tablespoons extra-virgin olive oil

1 Spanish onion, coarsely diced

Sea salt and freshly ground pepper

3 celery stalks, diced

2 cups dried red lentils, rinsed and
picked over

2 teaspoons smoked paprika

1 tablespoon ground cumin

4 cups low-sodium vegetable or
chicken broth

1 small sweet potato, baked (see
headnote)

1/2 teaspoon liquid smoke (optional)

1/2 cup chopped fresh cilantro

Juice of 1 small lemon or lime

Whole-milk Greek yogurt, for garnish

5 slices crisp cooked bacon, chopped,
for garnish (optional)

Heat the olive oil in a large pot over medium heat. Add the onion and
a big pinch of salt, stir, and cook until the onion is translucent, 5 to
8 minutes. Add the celery, stir, and cook until just softened, about
another 5 minutes.

Add the lentils, paprika, cumin, and broth. Bring everything to a
boil, then turn the heat back down to a simmer. Cover and simmer,
stirring occasionally, until the lentils are soft but not falling apart,
about 15 minutes.

Peel the baked sweet potato and add the flesh and liquid smoke to the
lentils. Using an immersion blender or blender, puree the soup until
it is just blended but still has a bit of texture left (don't overprocess
it). Taste and add more salt and pepper, if desired. Stir in half of the
cilantro and the lemon juice.

To serve, garnish with a dollop of Greek yogurt, a pinch of the
remaining cilantro, and the bacon. Serve hot.

All things considered,

this soup comes together quickly, and
most of the ingredients are things you
likely have in your cupboard. Lentils
make a great vegetarian meal because
they provide the protein, carbohydrates, and fiber to keep you satiated.
Because roasting a sweet potato takes
about 45 minutes, I will sometimes
make a couple in advance to have
them ready for meals during the week.
Prick each potato with a fork, wrap it in
foil, and roast it in the oven for about
45 minutes until you can easily pierce
to the middle with a knife. They keep
covered in the fridge for about a week.

All-natural liquid smoke is a great
addition to this soup, but it isn't critical, so feel free to eliminate it for the
sake of convenience. I've substituted
a can of coconut milk for some of the
broth before and the soup tastes a bit
creamier and barely sweeter, if you
like that sort of thing. This is a nice,
light soup, so be generous with your
garnishes. In addition to those listed
below, you could also use some diced
avocado or a drizzle of browned butter.

edamame dumplings

SERVES 4 <

WONTONS

4 green onions, white and green parts, coarsely chopped

2 tablespoons toasted sesame oil

1/4 cup fresh basil leaves, coarsely chopped

2 cups shelled edamame, cooked and drained

2 tablespoons regular or vegan sour cream

Dash of hot sauce

40 round wonton wrappers

BROTH

4 cups mushroom or low-sodium vegetable broth

1 lemongrass stalk

2 tablespoons mirin

2 tablespoons low-sodium soy sauce

Toasted sesame seeds, for garnish

Microgreens or pea shoots, for garnish

Combine the green onions, sesame oil, basil, edamame, sour cream, and hot sauce in a food processor. Process to a puree. On a lightly floured work surface, place a heaping tablespoonful of the edamame filling in the center of a wonton wrapper. Use your finger to wipe a bit of water around the edge of the wrapper. Place another wonton wrapper on top of the filling and press down along the edges to adhere. Repeat with remaining wrappers and filling.

To make the broth, warm the mushroom broth in a pot over medium-low heat. Pound the lemongrass with the back of a heavy knife to release its oils and discard the tough outer layer. Mince the inner, pale portion of the bottom of the stalk and add it to the broth along with the mirin and soy sauce. Gently simmer for 10 minutes to combine the flavors. Cover and turn the heat to low to keep warm. Add enough of the broth to a saucepan to cover the bottom, about 1 cup, and add a single layer of wontons (you will probably need to do this in two batches). Cover and steam over medium-low heat until the wontons are warmed, about 2 minutes.

To serve, divide the wontons among four shallow bowls and pour about 1/2 cup of the remaining broth on top. Garnish with a sprinkle of the toasted sesame seeds and sprouts and serve hot.

As someone who typically cooks quickly, I like the change of pace when I need to be delicate and thoughtful with a particular dish. This recipe is by no means a challenge, but it does take a bit of tenderness to craft each dumpling with just enough green filling to make a plump little pillow. I'm partial to making these in the shape of a ravioli using two wonton wrappers, as they lay so nicely in the broth. To make something smaller, you could fold one wonton wrapper in half over less filling.

The dumplings can be prepped an hour or two in advance, but the moist filling will soak through the wrapper a bit, which may cause them to tear. To minimize this problem, store them in the fridge on a parchment-lined baking sheet. I have just steamed them here, but if you sear them on each side in a bit of sesame oil before steaming them, the dumplings gets a crisp crust that adds some nice texture.

moroccan stuffed squash

SERVES 4 <

2 medium acorn squash

3 tablespoons coconut oil

Sea salt and freshly ground pepper

1 cup quinoa

1 (13.5-ounce) can light coconut milk

1 teaspoon sweet paprika

1/4 teaspoon ground coriander

1/4 teaspoon ground cumin

1/4 cup thinly sliced preserved lemon peel, or 2 tablespoons grated lemon zest

2 tablespoons chopped fresh mint

3 tablespoons chopped fresh cilantro

2 tablespoons freshly squeezed orange juice

1/2 cup pomegranate seeds

1/2 cup feta cheese, plus more for garnish

1/2 cup chopped toasted pistachios (optional)

Preheat the oven to 425°F. Cut the acorn squash in half lengthwise and scoop out the seeds. Rub 1 tablespoon of the coconut oil on the cut sides of the squash halves and sprinkle with salt and pepper. Place the squash, cut side down, on a baking sheet and pierce the skin a few times with a fork. Roast for 20 minutes. Flip them over and continue cooking, cut side up, until you can easily poke a knife through the flesh at its thickest part, another 10 to 20 minutes depending on its size. Remove from the oven and let cool.

While the squash are cooking, rinse the quinoa in a fine-mesh strainer. Bring the coconut milk to a gentle boil over medium-high heat, with a pinch of salt and pepper. Add the quinoa, turn the heat down to a simmer and cover. Cook until the liquid is absorbed, 15 to 18 minutes, then turn off the heat and let the quinoa steam in the pot for 5 minutes. Add the remaining 2 tablespoons coconut oil, the paprika, coriander, and cumin to the quinoa and toss to combine. Add the preserved lemon peel, mint, cilantro, orange juice, pomegranate seeds, and feta and toss together. Taste and add salt and pepper, if necessary.

Divide the mixture between the cavities of the squash. Garnish with a sprinkle of feta and the pistachios. Serve immediately.

I experimented with preserved lemons a year or so ago and found that as frequently as I use citrus, I couldn't quite figure out where to use them. They have just the slightest amount of puckery lemon flavor and more of a pickled flavor instead. I found they work best as a background flavor, as they add something unique that you can't quite put your finger on, like they do in the quinoa here. Scoop out the flesh of the lemon and discard it, using only the chopped rind. I know this is an offbeat ingredient, so please don't let it deter you from making this dish. There are instructions on page 229 if you'd like to make them yourself. Alternatively, a bit of lemon or orange zest will do just fine.

This dish can stand alone as a vegetarian entrée but would also make a great side dish if made with smaller acorn squash. If you want to prepare this in advance, you can make the quinoa stuffing up to two days ahead, mixing together everything but the feta. When you are ready to serve, warm the quinoa and toss in the feta before stuffing the squash.

roasted cauliflower capellini

SERVES 4 <

1 head cauliflower (about 3 pounds)

2 tablespoons extra-virgin olive oil

2 teaspoons lemon pepper

Sea salt and freshly ground pepper

1 teaspoon freshly grated nutmeg

1/2 pound whole grain or brown rice capellini or spaghetti

3 tablespoons unsalted butter

2 tablespoons white balsamic vinegar

Handful of fresh basil leaves, cut into thin slivers

1/2 cup chopped toasted hazelnuts

Shaved Pecorino, for garnish (optional)

Preheat the oven to 425°F.

Bring a large pot of salted water to a boil over high heat for the capellini. Meanwhile, cut the cauliflower into 1-inch florets, discarding the thick middle stem. Spread the florets on a rimmed baking sheet and toss with the olive oil, making sure each piece is coated. Sprinkle with the lemon pepper, 1/2 teaspoon of salt, and the nutmeg and toss again. Roast, gently stirring about halfway through the cooking time, until there are lots of brown caramelized spots, 25 to 30 minutes.

Cook the capellini according to the package instructions. Meanwhile, in a large sauté pan over medium heat, warm the butter and swirl it around the pan until it starts to bubble and just begins to smell toasty, about 2 minutes. Turn off the heat. Drain the pasta, reserving a bit of the water. To the pan with the browned butter, add the capellini, a splash of the pasta water, the balsamic vinegar, basil, half of both the cauliflower and the hazelnuts, and a pinch or two of salt and toss everything to combine. Divide the capellini among four bowls and top each serving with a portion of the remaining cauliflower and hazelnuts and a few grinds of pepper. Garnish with some shaved Pecorino and serve immediately.

I had been daydreaming about this combination for a few weeks, despite not being much for pasta dishes. I tried to paint a picture of this dish for Hugh, but he assured me that neither he nor the rest of the world liked cauliflower in any form. Still, I made it anyway. Would you guess who came back for seconds and has requested it since? The cauliflower is caramelized until it gives off a nice nutty smell, a hint of nutmeg lingers in the background, and a thin coating of brown butter makes the whole dish just rich enough without being heavy. If you want to keep it dairy-free, you can substitute hazelnut oil for the butter and still enjoy excellent flavor.

I prefer pasta as a side dish rather than a main course, but since I know there are pasta lovers (hey, Dad!), I'll let you make that decision on your own. You could serve this with some roasted chicken, perhaps put a poached egg on top, or stir in some cooked chickpeas for a bit of extra protein.

mushroom and brown rice veggie burgers

SERVES 6 <

2 tablespoons unsalted butter

5 cups stemmed and finely chopped cremini mushrooms (about 1 pound)

5 cloves garlic, chopped

Sea salt and freshly ground pepper

1/4 cup ground flaxseed (flax meal)

1/2 cup freshly grated Parmesan cheese

1 cup cooked chickpeas, drained well

3 Medjool dates, pitted

1/4 cup fresh flat-leaf parsley leaves

1 egg

1 teaspoon fennel seeds

2 1/2 tablespoons tahini

3 tablespoons tamari or soy sauce

2 cups cooked and cooled brown rice

1 to 2 tablespoons old-fashioned rolled oats, as needed

4 large shallots, sliced thin

1 teaspoon extra-virgin olive oil or coconut oil

6 whole grain English muffins

3/4 cup hummus (page 138)

2 avocados, peeled and sliced

2 cups arugula

Melt the butter in a large sauté pan. Add the mushrooms, garlic, and a pinch of salt and sauté until the mushrooms are softened and the excess water has cooked off, 8 to 10 minutes. Turn off the heat and set aside to cool.

Combine the ground flaxseed, Parmesan, chickpeas, dates, parsley, egg, fennel seeds, tahini, tamari, 1/2 teaspoon of salt, and 1 teaspoon of pepper in a food processor. Give the mixture a few pulses to combine well and transfer to a large mixing bowl. Once the mushrooms are at room temperature, add them, along with any juices in the pan, to the bowl along with the rice and stir to combine. Cover and refrigerate for about 30 minutes. At this point the mixture should be pretty moist, but if it seems too wet to form into a patty, stir in 1 to 2 tablespoons of oats to soak up some of the moisture. The recipe can be prepared to this point up to a day in advance.

(continued)

I try to stay abreast of all things burger, as I am married to someone who eats them quite frequently. There was a great article in the *New York Times* last year about restaurants that had attempted to create the perfect veggie burger, boasting their secret recipes so tasty that carnivores wouldn't miss the meat. I tested this recipe about seven times before I felt it was worth sharing, since veggie burgers often land somewhere between dry, crumbly, and bland homemade versions and store-bought patties full of unnatural ingredients. You may look at the lengthy ingredients list and turn the page, but I assure you that there is some depth here, some umami, if you will, that is worth the trip to the market. It takes some time to get the ingredients to achieve the right texture, where the patty will stick together but every ingredient is still just distinguishable. I bake mine, as I find them too delicate and moist to pan-fry, but if you prefer a crisp crust, that is certainly your call. This burger goes great sandwiched between the halves of a thin, crisp English muffin or served open-faced with lots of peppery arugula on top. If you don't have shallots around, a red onion would be a fine substitute.

Arrange a rack in the upper third of your oven and preheat the oven to 475°F.

Form the mixture into 6 patties, each about 1 inch thick. Line a baking sheet with parchment paper or a nonstick silicone baking mat and arrange the patties on the baking sheet with space in between. Bake them in the oven until toasted on top, 14 to 18 minutes.

While the burgers cook, prepare the shallots. Warm the oil in a sauté pan over medium heat. Add the shallots and a pinch of salt and sauté until the edges begin to brown, 5 to 7 minutes. Set aside for assembly.

After removing the patties from the oven, toast the English muffins while the burgers rest for a moment. Put a swipe of hummus on each muffin half and assemble the burgers by layering the patty, avocado slices, arugula, and the sautéed shallots. Serve immediately.

Tahini is a sesame paste that can be found in the ethnic aisle or near the nut butters at your local health food store.

creamy millet with roasted portobellos

SERVES 4 <

1 cup millet

2 1/2 cups milk

Sea salt and freshly ground pepper

1/2 teaspoon freshly grated nutmeg

2 tablespoons fresh thyme leaves

1/2 to 3/4 cup grated Pecorino cheese, plus more for garnish

1/4 cup crumbled Gorgonzola

4 portobello mushrooms, stemmed

2 tablespoons extra-virgin olive oil

2 tablespoons white balsamic vinegar

2 teaspoons herbes de Provence

1 bunch lacinato (Tuscan) kale, stemmed and coarsely chopped

Pinch of red pepper flakes (optional)

Preheat the oven to 400°F. Rinse and drain the millet. Put it in a heavy pot (enameled cast-iron, if you have one). Add the milk, 2 cups water, and a big pinch of salt. Stir. Bring to a boil over medium-high heat, then reduce to a gentle simmer, cover, and cook, stirring occasionally so the bottom doesn't burn, until tender, 20 to 25 minutes. Stir in the nutmeg and thyme and cook another 3 minutes. The consistency should be like that of a soft polenta with some millet nuggets in it. If it starts to thicken too much or the texture is too coarse, add another 1/2 cup water as it cooks. Stir in both cheeses, taste, and add salt and pepper, if desired. Turn off the heat and leave the lid ajar.

In a large bowl, stir together the oil, vinegar, herbes de Provence, and 1/2 teaspoon of salt. Brush both sides of the mushrooms with the dressing and gently toss the kale with the remaining dressing. Put the mushrooms on a rimmed baking sheet, stem side up. Bake until the mushrooms have shrunk down and softened, 10 to 12 minutes. Remove the baking sheet from the oven, spread the kale in the remaining space, sprinkle with the red pepper flakes, and roast until the kale is just softened and crisped a bit, another 5 minutes.

To serve, place a generous scoop of the cheesy millet on each plate. Top with a portobello, some roasted kale, some Pecorino, and serve.

When I make a vegetarian entrée, it is always in the back of my mind that a minority of people eat this way, so I try to come up with things that are interesting and balanced for a vegetarian but that someone who does eat meat would find filling, or at least a satisfying side dish to their protein of choice.

I try to use kale often, as its nutritional profile is quite impressive. In this dish, its short time in the oven helps it to retain most of its structure, but make sure that the oil really coats the kale, since if you use too little you will get something more like kale chips. If you use curly kale, which is less tender than lacinato kale, or you prefer your greens more wilted, you could sauté it quickly instead. I use lots of liquid in the millet, so the result is nice and soft but bound together by the sharply flavored cheese. The bits of millet are still detectable, but it has a comfort food texture. Whether you serve it as an entrée or a side is up to you.

lentil meatballs with lemon pesto

SERVES 4 <

1 cup lentils, rinsed

2 cups water

2 eggs, lightly beaten

1 tablespoon extra-virgin olive oil

³/₄ cup ricotta

¹/₄ cup freshly grated Parmesan cheese

2 cloves garlic, minced

¹/₂ teaspoon fennel seeds

2 tablespoons chopped fresh flat-leaf parsley

Few pinches of fresh thyme leaves or dried thyme

1 teaspoon sea salt

1 teaspoon freshly ground pepper

²/₃ cup bread crumbs

LEMON PESTO SAUCE

1 clove garlic

¹/₄ cup pine nuts

Grated zest and juice of 1 Meyer lemon

Pinch of sea salt

1 cup packed fresh basil leaves

¹/₄ to ¹/₃ cup extra-virgin olive oil

2 tablespoons freshly grated Parmesan cheese

2 tablespoons water

If a food could be both hearty and light at the same time, these lentil meatballs would be it. We make them into a hearty meal by serving them on a bed of quinoa, noodles, or sautéed greens, but they're also convenient to have on hand for a quick lunch on their own under a blanket of the bright, citrusy pesto.

I have provided instructions for cooking the lentils, but using 2 cups from a prepared package of steamed lentils will save you a step.

Put the lentils in a pot with the water and bring to a gentle boil over medium-high heat. Reduce the heat to a simmer and cook, uncovered, until the lentils are tender, 15 to 20 minutes, adding water if the liquid has evaporated and the lentils are still tough. Drain the lentils and set aside to cool.

Transfer the lentils to a food processor and pulse until it forms a chunky puree. Transfer to a large mixing bowl and add the eggs, olive oil, ricotta, Parmesan, garlic, fennel seeds, parsley, thyme, salt, and pepper. Stir to combine well. Stir in the bread crumbs and let sit at room temperature for 15 minutes to allow the flavors to blend.

Preheat the oven to 400°F and line a rimmed baking sheet with parchment paper.

In the meantime, make your pesto. In a food processor or mini blender, blend the garlic, pine nuts, lemon, and salt until smooth.

Add the basil, 1/4 cup of the olive oil, and Parmesan and pulse again until smooth, adding more olive oil as needed to smooth it out and a bit of water as needed to get a thinner, saucelike consistency.

Check the lentil mixture by rolling a 1-inch ball together between your palms; it should hold together fairly well. If it seems too wet, add another tablespoon or two of the bread crumbs to the mixture. Roll the lentil mixture into 1-inch balls and arrange them on the prepared baking sheet. They don't need a lot of space between. If you like a bit more of a crust, give them a thin brush of olive oil. Bake until the tops are golden brown, gently turning the balls over halfway through, 15 to 20 minutes. Remove to cool slightly.

Serve with a drizzle of pesto sauce.

buckwheat harvest tart

SERVES 6 <

CRUST

1 cup buckwheat flour

3/4 cup unbleached all-purpose flour

1/2 teaspoon sea salt

1/2 cup cold unsalted butter, cut into cubes

2 teaspoons fresh thyme leaves

1 tablespoon apple cider vinegar

2 to 3 tablespoons cold water

FILLING

3 cups cubed butternut squash (1/4-inch cubes)

2 tablespoons extra-virgin olive oil

Sea salt and freshly ground black pepper

1/2 teaspoon freshly grated nutmeg

2 cloves garlic, minced

1 bunch Swiss chard, stems removed, coarsely chopped (about 6 cups chopped)

1/2 teaspoon red pepper flakes

1 small yellow onion

2 tablespoons balsamic vinegar

3 eggs

1 cup grated Gruyère

To make the crust, in a food processor, add both flours and the salt and pulse to combine. Add the butter and thyme and pulse until pea-size chunks form. Keep pulsing while adding the vinegar and then the cold water, 1 tablespoon at a time, stopping when the dough just barely holds together. Form the dough into a disk, wrap it in plastic wrap, and chill in the fridge for at least 30 minutes or up to overnight.

Preheat the oven to 400°F.

On a lightly floured surface, roll out the dough into a 13-inch circle. It should be about 1/4 inch thick. Roll the dough around the rolling pin and lift it into an 11-inch fluted tart pan with a removable bottom. Press the dough into the edges and up the sides, making sure to patch up any holes. Gently roll your rolling pin across the top of the tart pan to remove the extra dough and create a clean edge. Prick the bottom of the dough with a fork, lay a piece of parchment paper on top, and fill the tart shell with pie weights (I use rocks from the yard—classy, I know). Bake for 15 minutes. Remove the parchment and weights and bake until the top looks almost dry, another 10 to 12 minutes. Remove from the oven and let cool.

After Hugh and I got married, just before I started writing this book, I started experimenting with vegetable dishes that could qualify as "man food." I came up with this dish featuring the fabulous combination of barely sweet squash and savory onions. At that point I could count on one hand how many times I had made a tart, so I was pleasantly surprised when this went over as well as it did.

I will not lie; this tart has a fair number of steps and will leave you with a sink full of dishes, but it's worth it. If you like, you can make the tart shell, roast the squash, and sauté the chard a day in advance, then bring everything to room temperature before assembling it. Make sure that there are no holes in the tart crust and that it is completely cooled before adding the filling. I've had the egg mixture leak through the crust before, so hopefully I'm sparing you the same frustration.

While the crust is cooling, prepare the filling. On a rimmed baking sheet, toss the squash with 1/2 tablespoon of the olive oil, 1/2 teaspoon salt, and the nutmeg. Spread in an even layer and bake until the squash begins to brown around the edges, 20 to 25 minutes. Remove from the oven and let cool.

In a large sauté pan over medium heat, warm 1 tablespoon of the olive oil and the garlic. When the garlic starts to sizzle a bit and becomes fragrant, add the Swiss chard, red pepper flakes, and a pinch of salt. Sauté until the chard is wilted, about 5 minutes. Transfer to a large mixing bowl and set aside.

Peel and halve the onion and thinly slice. In the same pan you used for the chard, heat the remaining 1/2 tablespoon olive oil over medium heat. Add the onion and a pinch of salt and stir every so often until caramelized, about 20 minutes. When the onions are a nice light brown color, add the balsamic vinegar, stir, and turn off the heat. The onions will absorb the vinegar as they cool a bit.

Squeeze out any excess water from the Swiss chard and return to the bowl. In a separate bowl, whisk the eggs until blended well, then add to the chard. To the bowl with the chard, add three-fourths of the squash, half of the cheese, the onion, and a few grinds of black pepper. Gently mix everything together and pour into the tart pan. Spread into an even layer. Scatter the remaining squash and cheese across the top. Bake in the oven until the egg is just set and the top is browned, 24 to 28 minutes. Remove the tart from the oven and allow it to cool for 5 to 10 minutes before cutting into slices and serving.

This can also be made in a springform pan if you don't have a fluted tart pan. Because many springform pans are about 9 inches around, the crust will be a bit thicker, so be sure to press the dough gently up the sides of the pan in an even layer, just as you would the tart pan. The filling will be a tad deeper too, so add a few minutes to the final baking time.

grilled flatbreads with pear, arugula, and goat cheese

MAKES 4 SMALL OR 2 LARGE FLATBREADS <

CRUST

1 teaspoon active dry yeast

1 teaspoon honey

1½ cups Tipo 00 pizza flour or unbleached all-purpose flour

1½ cups spelt flour

1 teaspoon sea salt

2 tablespoons extra-virgin olive oil

3 teaspoons extra-virgin olive oil

1 yellow onion, thinly sliced

2 firm but ripe red pears

3 tablespoons whole grain mustard

1 cup fresh goat cheese (about 8 ounces)

Sea salt and freshly ground pepper

3 cups baby arugula

1 tablespoon balsamic vinegar

Put the yeast and honey in a bowl with ¼ cup warm water (no warmer than 100°F). Let sit for about 10 minutes; the mixture should start to bubble slightly. Mix both flours and the salt in a large bowl, add the yeast mixture and olive oil to the bowl, and stir to combine. Add 1 cup warm water and knead with your hands until the dough is smooth, adding more water, 1 tablespoon at a time, if the dough feels too dry. Brush the dough with the olive oil, put it in a bowl, and cover with a dish towel. Let it rise at least 1 hour until it is double in size.

Remove the dough from the bowl. Punch it down to remove the air and knead it a few more times. Put it back in the bowl, cover with the dish towel, and leave it to rise again for another hour. Divide the dough into two or four portions, roll them into balls and let them rise, yes, another hour while covered in the bowl.

In between rises, caramelize the onion. Heat 2 teaspoons of the olive oil in a large skillet over medium heat, add the onion, and cook until light brown, 20 to 25 minutes. Core the pears and slice into thin wedges.

(continued)

Making your own pizza dough may seem time consuming, but it spends most of its time resting. Start it early in the day and just visit it between errands and again when you're home from work. (I brought a dough ball to work once, before I realized how flexible the rising times were. I never was the cool kid, so not much damage was done to my reputation, but I don't suggest you do this as it's completely unnecessary.) Come mealtime, you'll be proud you made it yourself. In a pinch, I would recommend going to a local pizza shop versus buying something at the store. They will typically sell you freshly made dough at an affordable price.

The "Tipo 00" flour used in this recipe can be found in specialty food stores and online. One of the most reputable brands is Molino Caputo. It is unique because of its fine grind, although it still has about 12 percent high-quality gluten. This flour creates a supple, stretchable dough that makes a great crust. If you don't have any, it's not a crucial element—unbleached all-purpose flour or bread flour would be a fine alternative.

(grilled flatbreads with pear, arugula, and goat cheese, continued)

Heat up your grill or grill pan over medium-high heat, making sure the grill grates are very clean to avoid sticking. If you're using a grill pan, preheat your broiler as well.

Roll out the dough balls as thinly as possible and grill on each side until grill marks are visible, about 3 minutes. Transfer the flatbreads to a wire rack. On each flatbread, divide and layer the toppings: spread the mustard, followed by a layer of goat cheese, the caramelized onions, and the pears. Sprinkle the flatbreads with a bit of pepper and put them back on the grill or under the broiler until cooked through and cheese is just melted, 6 to 8 minutes. Transfer them again to the wire racks; this prevents the steam from making the dough soggy. Toss the arugula with the balsamic vinegar, the remaining 1 teaspoon olive oil, and a pinch of salt and pepper. Top the pizzas with the arugula, slice, and serve hot.

roasted wild cod with meyer lemon and caper relish

SERVES 4 <

1 Meyer or Eureka lemon

Sea salt and freshly ground pepper

3 tablespoons champagne vinegar

2 tablespoons agave nectar

4 (5-ounce) wild cod fillets

2 shallots, minced (about 3 tablespoons)

$^1/_3$ cup capers, rinsed, drained, and coarsely chopped

3 tablespoons finely chopped fresh flat-leaf parsley

3 tablespoons extra-virgin olive oil

1 tablespoon coconut oil

2 tablespoons unsalted butter

Start the lemons preferably a day before and no fewer than four hours before you plan to serve the dish. Cut both ends off the lemon, cut in halve lengthwise, and remove the seeds. Use a sharp knife to cut into thin wedges and then finely dice. Add the lemon pieces to a bowl with any juices that have puddled on the cutting board. Add 1 teaspoon of salt, the vinegar, and agave nectar and stir. Cover with plastic wrap and leave at room temperature for at least 4 hours and up to overnight.

Remove the fish from the fridge, pat dry, and leave on a plate to allow to come to room temperature. Arrange a rack in the top third of your oven and preheat the oven to 400°F.

Add the shallots, capers, parsley, and olive oil to the bowl with the lemon mixture and stir to combine. The mixture should be pretty wet.

Season both sides of the fish with salt and pepper. Warm the coconut oil and 1 tablespoon of the butter in a large ovenproof skillet over medium-high heat and swirl to coat the bottom of the pan. Once warm, add the fish fillets to the pan without touching each other. Sear until the bottom of each fillet is just golden, about 2 minutes, and gently flip to sear the second side, about another 2 minutes.

(continued)

A light white fish served with a mango avocado salsa was once my go-to combination when I wanted to prepare fish. But when friends began asking me for easy fish ideas, and I realized I didn't tend to stray too far from my norm, I started experimenting with this Mediterranean combination. The Meyer lemon and caper relish, which is similar in texture to a salsa or pico de gallo, has both acidity and sweetness, and it adds moisture and excellent flavor to the fish. It takes some planning, but starting the relish the day or the morning before serving it will allow the lemons to soften. Be sure to use Meyer or Eureka lemons, which are generally available in the winter and early spring, because they have thinner skin and a sweeter flavor than other types, which are too tart for this recipe. Soaked in the lemon juice and vinegar, the lemon rind will "quick-preserve" itself and calm down, making it less bitter and more pleasant to eat. This recipe will work with any white fish, though you'll have to adjust the cooking time based on the fat content and thickness of the fillets.

Spoon the lemon relish on top of each fillet, allowing the liquid from the relish to drip into the pan as well. Add the remaining 1 tablespoon of butter to the pan and put it in the oven until the fish reaches the desired doneness. For fillets that are around 1 1/2 inches thick, allow about 6 minutes for medium doneness. You can test it by pressing on the center; it should resist just a little bit. Alternatively, see if you can easily flake the middle of the fillet with a fork.

Remove the fish from the oven. Carefully place each fillet and the lemon relish that is on top of it onto a plate and drizzle with a bit of the pan sauce. Sprinkle with a few grinds of pepper and serve warm.

soba bowls with tea-poached salmon

SERVES 4 <

3 tablespoons toasted sesame oil

2 tablespoons tahini

2 tablespoons agave nectar

Grated zest and juice of 1 lime

3 tablespoons tamari or soy sauce

2-inch piece of fresh ginger, peeled and finely grated

1 bunch broccoli

2 teaspoons extra-virgin olive oil

1 clove garlic, minced

Pinch of sea salt

3 bags green tea

1 tablespoon peppercorns

1/2 cup mirin or dry white wine

1 1/4 pound wild salmon fillet

1 (9.5-ounce) package soba noodles

4 green onions, white and green parts, thinly sliced on the diagonal

1/2 cup coarsely chopped fresh cilantro

1/4 cup white or black sesame seeds

Preheat the oven to 425°F.

In a small bowl, whisk together the sesame oil, tahini, agave nectar, lime zest and juice, tamari, and grated ginger until smooth. Set aside.

Cut the broccoli into small florets, including some of the stems. Combine the broccoli in a bowl with the olive oil, garlic, and salt and spread on a rimmed baking sheet. Roast for 15 minutes, then remove from the oven.

In a saucepan, bring 1 cup water to a gentle simmer. Turn the heat down to low, add the tea bags and peppercorns and steep for 3 minutes, then discard the tea bags. Add the mirin to the poaching liquid. Gently slide in the salmon, skin side down. Cover, and cook until the salmon is just barely cooked in the middle, 8 to 10 minutes, depending on the thickness of the fillet. If in doubt, it's better to undercook the salmon a bit rather than overcook it. Remove the salmon to a plate and flake it with a fork (you will notice a natural grain). Set aside and loosely cover with foil.

I never thought about it until I overheard Hugh's response to a friend's question about my cooking style. "She likes bowl foods," he said, "a lot of good flavors and textures together in a bowl." After I got over being offended (I mean, really, "bowl foods"? That isn't a style for heaven's sake!), I realized he was absolutely right. It may be the newlywed in me, but we often find ourselves eating dinner on the couch or wanting to sit on the floor and start a movie while we enjoy our food. How much easier is it to have everything in one bowl? Your vegetables, protein, and grain all in one vessel, one utensil, fewer dishes . . . it just seems efficient to me some nights. This meal actually requires using a number of dishes to get to the "bowl food" part, but you catch my drift. You'll need to prep most of the ingredients first, since once you start to poach the salmon and cook the noodles, everything moves pretty quickly. A few of the tasks can be done simultaneously. If you don't have a lime, it tastes great with the juice of a mandarin or half an orange as well. If you like lots of sauce, I'd double the quantity for good measure. Substituting sautéed tofu for the salmon makes an easy vegetarian alternative.

Meanwhile, bring a large pot of salted water to a boil. Cook the soba noodles according to package instructions or until al dente. While the noodles cook, chop the roasted broccoli. Drain the noodles. In a large bowl, toss together the warm noodles, broccoli, dressing, green onions, and half the cilantro. Divide the noodles among four bowls, top with a portion of the salmon, and sprinkle the remaining cilantro and the sesame seeds on top. Serve immediately.

walnut-crusted wild salmon with edamame mash

SERVES 4 <

3 1/2 cups frozen shelled edamame

Sea salt and freshly ground pepper

2 tablespoons rice vinegar

2 tablespoons freshly squeezed lemon juice

1 to 2 tablespoons toasted sesame oil, as needed (optional)

3 tablespoons chopped fresh chives, plus more for garnish

1 tablespoon chopped fresh mint

1 tablespoon grated ginger or 1/2 teaspoon red pepper flakes (optional)

1 egg white

1/4 cup whole wheat or rice flour

1 cup walnuts, very finely chopped

1 teaspoon dried basil

1 tablespoon coconut oil or grapeseed oil

4 (4-ounce) wild salmon fillets, skin removed

Preheat the oven to 400°F.

Steam or boil the edamame beans until softened, about 8 minutes. Drain the beans and transfer to a food processor or blender. Add a pinch of salt and pepper, the rice vinegar, lemon juice, and 1 table-spoon of sesame oil. Pulse the beans until fairly smooth but still slightly chunky, adding a little sesame oil or water as necessary to loosen it. Transfer to a bowl, add the chives and mint, and stir to combine. Add salt and pepper to taste. Stir in the ground ginger or red pepper flakes if you want a kick.

Combine the egg white and 1 tablespoon water in a bowl and whisk. Put the egg white mixture in a shallow bowl and the flour in a second shallow bowl. In a third shallow bowl, stir together the walnuts, a pinch of salt, and the basil. Heat the coconut oil in a large ovenproof pan over medium heat. Working with one piece of salmon at a time, dip one side of the fillet in the flour, then the egg white, then the walnuts, which should be chopped finely enough to adhere. Repeat with the remaining fillets. Place the fillets, crust side down, gently in the pan and sear for about 3 minutes, then flip and sear the other

You'll want to choose

a wild variety of salmon, for both health reasons and sustainability— farming salmon requires a larger amount of wild fish to feed the farmed ones, making the process unsustainable. You can find wild salmon at a fish market, a natural foods market, or a well-stocked grocery store. Fish have seasons just like produce does, and although you can typically find it year-round, salmon season peaks in midsummer. There are a number of varieties, all quite rich, so a small portion suffices for most people. If salmon isn't your thing, you could use another fish, varying the cooking time if you are using a thinner fillet or a less fatty variety of fish.

The edamame mash has a nice toasty flavor from the sesame oil that complements the nuts crusting the fish. And about that crust . . . it has a humble crunch that nicely offsets the tender fish inside and the smooth bed of mash it sits on. This could pass as dinner for company that won't take you all day to prepare.

side, about 2 minutes more. Put the pan in the oven and cook until the salmon reaches the desired doneness, 4 to 5 minutes.

On each plate, put a generous dollop of the edamame mash and place the warm salmon on top. Garnish with chives and serve.

green herb shrimp with summer squash couscous

SERVES 4 <

HERB SAUCE

1/4 cup extra-virgin olive oil

1/2 teaspoon sea salt

4 green onions, white and light green parts, chopped

2 tablespoons coarsely chopped fresh mint leaves

1/2 cup coarsely chopped fresh basil

1/2 cup fresh flat-leaf parsley

2 cloves garlic

2 anchovies (optional)

Juice of 2 limes

1 1/2 pounds large shrimp, peeled and deveined

1 1/2 tablespoon extra virgin olive oil

4 cups diced zucchini (about 4 medium)

1 1/2 cups whole wheat couscous

1/4 cup coarsely chopped fresh basil

1/2 teaspoon red pepper flakes

1/3 cup diced feta cheese

2 tablespoons red wine vinegar

Sea salt and freshly ground pepper

In a food processor or blender, combine all of the sauce ingredients and blend until fairly smooth with a few herb flecks. Put half of the sauce in a bowl along with the shrimp and set aside to marinate for 1 hour, reserving the other half of the sauce.

Heat 1/2 tablespoon of the oil in a cast-iron pan or large skillet over medium heat. Add the zucchini and sauté until the edges are browned, 8 to 10 minutes.

Cook the couscous according to the package instructions. Transfer the couscous to a large mixing bowl and add the zucchini, the remaining 1 tablespoon of oil, the basil, red pepper flakes, feta, and vinegar. Toss to coat. Add salt and pepper to taste.

Heat a grill or grill pan over high heat. Cook the shrimp until they just turn pink, about 2 minutes maximum on each side; be careful to avoid overcooking them. Toss the cooked shrimp in the remaining herb sauce and serve with the zucchini couscous.

While this sauce is excellent on the shrimp here, it is also my go-to condiment for lots of other ingredients. I like to put it on top of grilled fish fillets or mix it into any kind of cooked grain and add some sturdy greens for a nice salad. I also love it on an open-faced sandwich with some tomatoes and melty cheese. I'm an easy sell when it comes to herbs and citrus, whose versatility never ceases to amaze me.

This bowl of goodness is pretty easily adapted to your protein of choice. You can use some tofu or tempeh if you want to keep it vegetarian. The zucchini shrinks down quite a bit, so if you like your couscous with lots of vegetables, up the quantity of zucchini a touch and add a bit more oil and vinegar to the finished dish.

Remember to check the Seafood Watch list (see page 13) when buying your shrimp!

seared scallops on black quinoa with pomegranate gastrique

SERVES 4 <

16 large scallops

1 cup black quinoa

1¹/₂ cups low-sodium vegetable broth

1 medium fennel bulb

2 tablespoons extra-virgin
   olive oil

¹/₄ cup finely chopped fresh chives,
   plus more for garnish

Sea salt and freshly ground pepper

2 tablespoons coconut oil or ghee, or
   more as needed

1 cup pomegranate seeds

Handful of microgreens

POMEGRANATE GASTRIQUE

1 tablespoon honey

2 tablespoons sherry vinegar

1 cup pomegranate juice

³/₄ cup low-sodium vegetable broth

Remove the scallops from the fridge to rest at room temperature.

To make the gastrique, in a saucepan over medium heat, warm the honey and vinegar, stirring to combine. Add the pomegranate juice, bring the mixture to a gentle boil, and cook until reduced by half, about 8 minutes. Add the vegetable broth and reduce in half again, another 6 to 8 minutes. Set aside to cool.

Rinse the quinoa in a fine-mesh strainer. In a saucepan, bring the vegetable broth to a simmer over medium heat, add the quinoa, cover, and cook until the liquid is absorbed, 16 to 18 minutes. While the quinoa is cooking, remove the fronds from the fennel and reserve a small handful. Core and slice the fennel bulb as thinly as possible, using a mandoline if you have one. Coarsely chop the reserved fronds. Once the quinoa is cooked, transfer it to a mixing bowl. Add the fronds, the sliced fennel bulb, olive oil, and chives to the quinoa and stir.

Pat the scallops completely dry and sprinkle all sides with salt and pepper. Heat the coconut oil in a large frying pan over medium-high

(continued)

I don't often approach cooking with many rules. Opinions certainly, but not rules. But scallops are one ingredient that I find benefits from the following three easy rules: always use fresh, not previously frozen, scallops; cook them the day of purchase; and cook your dry scallops in a hot liquid or fat for a good sear. This gorgeous recipe is the kind of dinner you could make for company, thanks to the beautiful black quinoa salad studded with teeny jewels of tart pomegranate seeds. I find that scallops have a creaminess that contrasts particularly well with the tart gastrique, but the sweet, acidic flavors are versatile enough to go with any protein. If you don't care for scallops, grill up some tofu spears, chicken breasts, or flank steak. Fresh seafood deteriorates quickly, so I suggest seeking out a reputable fishmonger and cooking the scallops as soon as you can. Any pieces with a shiny film or a "fishy" smell aren't fresh. The gastrique can be made a day in advance; after that, this recipe comes together fairly quickly. I use black quinoa for aesthetic reasons, but you could use the white or red variety instead. If you're wanting a bit of a salty bite, toss some finely crumbled feta into the quinoa.

heat and add as many scallops as will fit in the pan while leaving 1 to 2 inches between them. Cook for 4 minutes, flip, and cook on the other side until a crust has formed and the scallop starts to pull away from the pan, about 2 to 3 minutes more, depending on the size of the scallops. The key to getting a good crust on the scallops is to make sure they are close to room temperature and completely dry when they hit the hot pan. Don't touch them besides flipping them once. There is no need to stir them around; that's when things get messy. Repeat with the remaining scallops, adding a bit more coconut oil to the pan if it all has been absorbed.

Stir the pomegranate seeds and microgreens into the quinoa mixture, adding a few pinches of salt and pepper to taste.

To serve, divide the quinoa salad and scallops among four plates and drizzle each serving with the gastrique. Garnish with chives and serve immediately.

chipotle and apple turkey burgers

SERVES 4 <

HERB AIOLI

1 egg yolk

2 teaspoons freshly squeezed lemon juice

1/2 teaspoon sea salt

1/2 teaspoon freshly ground pepper

3/4 cup rice bran oil or canola oil

1 tablespoon Dijon mustard

2 tablespoons finely chopped fresh chives

2 tablespoons finely chopped fresh basil leaves

TURKEY BURGERS

1 tablespoon extra-virgin olive oil

1 celery stalk, finely chopped

3 green onions, finely chopped

4 cloves garlic, finely chopped

1 apple, such as Granny Smith or Gala

1 pound ground turkey

1 scant teaspoon chipotle chile powder, or 1 canned chipotle chile in adobo sauce, finely chopped

1/2 teaspoon sea salt

1/2 teaspoon freshly ground pepper

2 tablespoons fresh thyme leaves, chopped fresh chives, or chopped fresh flat-leaf parsley

FOR SERVING

4 slices provolone cheese

4 whole grain hamburger buns

1/2 head butter lettuce

1/2 cup caramelized onions (page 227)

1 beefsteak tomato, sliced

To make the aioli, wrap the bottom of a large bowl with a damp dish towel to help keep it in place. In the bowl, whisk together the egg yolk, lemon juice, salt, and pepper. Whisk in a few drops of the oil to establish an emulsion. While you continue to quickly whisk the mixture with one hand, slowly stream in the rest of the oil with the other. Once you have a mayonnaise-like consistency, whisk in the mustard, chives, and basil. Cover and store in the fridge until ready to use.

To make the burgers, heat the olive oil in a sauté pan. Add the celery, green onions, and garlic and sauté until just browned, about 5 minutes. Turn off the heat and set aside to cool.

(continued)

I tested these turkey burgers quite a few times before finding a balance. The bits of apple, celery, and onions give the burgers some texture while making them less dense, and the aioli and toppings keep them moist and flavorful. I typically serve this with the Spiced Sweet Potato Wedges (page 88) and the Honey Mustard Broccoli Salad (page 76), and for those who are watching their carbs, I serve it on a bed of tender greens.

Here I describe how to make the aioli by hand. You can also make it in a food processor, if you prefer. An even quicker shortcut would be to add the mustard and herbs to your favorite brand of mayonnaise. I know there is some controversy about the healthfulness of canola oil. However, an aioli made from olive oil alone will be strong tasting and "heavy," for lack of a better description. If you choose to use olive oil, it will still result in a creamy sauce, but it won't really resemble traditional aioli.

Using the large holes on a box grater, grate the apple. Combine the grated apple, turkey, chipotle, salt, pepper, thyme, and cooked vegetables in a large mixing bowl and stir everything together. Form the mixture into four patties, each 1½ inches thick, and let them rest at room temperature for about 15 minutes, or keep them covered in the fridge until ready to grill.

Heat your grill to medium-high. Cook the burgers until the interior reaches 175°F on an instant-read thermometer, about 5 minutes on each side. Put a slice of cheese on top of each patty in the last minute of cooking time to melt. Transfer the patties to a plate and cover loosely with foil.

Grill or toast the buns. Spread each side of the buns with a bit of aioli and layer with a piece of lettuce, a turkey burger, some caramelized onions, and a slice of tomato. Serve immediately.

greek grilled chicken with tzatziki

SERVES 4 <

MARINADE

1 cup whole-milk Greek yogurt

Grated zest and juice of 1 Meyer
    lemon

2 teaspoons ground cumin

2 tablespoons coarsely chopped fresh
    mint leaves

2 tablespoons coarsely chopped
    fresh dill

1 teaspoon dried oregano

1 teaspoon sea salt

1 teaspoon freshly ground pepper

4 boneless, skinless chicken breasts

TZATZIKI

2 English cucumbers

$1/4$ red onion, finely chopped

2 tablespoons finely chopped fresh
    mint leaves

2 tablespoons finely chopped fresh dill

1 clove garlic, minced

$1/3$ cup whole-milk Greek yogurt

3 tablespoons freshly squeezed lemon
    juice

Sea salt and freshly ground pepper

To make the marinade, mix all of the marinade ingredients together
in a shallow baking dish. Working with two chicken breasts at a time,
place them between two pieces of plastic wrap and pound them to
an even thickness of about $1/2$ inch. Put the chicken in the dish with
the marinade and turn so that it is fully coated. Let marinate at room
temperature for at least 15 minutes, or for a few hours in the fridge.

To make the tzatziki, slice each cucumber in half lengthwise. Use
a small spoon to scoop out the seeds in the center. Slice each half
lengthwise into four or five long sticks, then dice. You should have
about 3 cups.In a mixing bowl, stir together the cucumbers, red
onion, mint, dill, and garlic. Add the yogurt, lemon juice, $1/2$ teaspoon
of salt, and pepper to taste. Taste and adjust the seasonings as
desired. This is what gives flavor to a very lean piece of chicken, so
don't skimp on the flavors here.

This dish looks fabulous as
part of a dinner spread, with nice grill
marks on the chicken and all those
fresh, crunchy cucumbers on top.
I serve it with a side of quinoa with
chopped-up grilled lemon slices and
toasted pine nuts or some warm jas-
mine rice. The yogurt used to marinate
the chicken tenderizes it and helps all
the flavors really stick.

Note that although the chicken can be
marinated for a few hours, the cucumbers start to release water as soon as
they are mixed with salt, so I don't
suggest making the cucumber mixture too far in advance. You can mix
together the cucumber, herbs, and
onion in advance, if you like, but stir in
the yogurt and salt at the last minute.

Heat your grill to medium-high heat, making sure the grates are clean. Grill the chicken until the internal temperature reaches 180°F on an instant-read thermometer, about 4 minutes per side. Let the chicken rest for a few minutes before serving each breast with a large scoop of the tzatziki.

4

Snacks to Share

This is the chapter with the in-between dishes: those that are not quite a meal for guests but can certainly qualify as lunch most days. I prefer eating a number of small meals each day as opposed to a full spread, so these recipes are what keep me fueled. From the glove compartment of my car, to my purse, to my desk (which, yes, is just downstairs from the kitchen), I am fully stocked up on snacks. It's helpful to have nutritionally dense options handy to keep my energy up, and my preparedness has assisted many a friend in a moment of low blood sugar.

There are vegan wraps, which are easy to pack for work or a road trip, a coconut loaf to have on hand for when friends stop by, and some protein-packed nuts for grazing during the day. I enjoy both experimenting and using up whatever ingredients I have on hand, and that creativity and resourcefulness is the source of this collection of snacks.

quinoa collard wraps with miso-carrot spread

MAKES 4 <

MISO-CARROT SPREAD

1 cup coarsely chopped carrots

1 tablespoon fresh grated ginger

1 small shallot, chopped

1 tablespoon white or yellow miso

1 teaspoon honey

3 tablespoons rice vinegar

3 tablespoons toasted sesame oil

1/4 teaspoon sea salt

8 large collard green leaves

2 cups cooked quinoa (see page 231)

1 tablespoon tahini

Freshly squeezed lemon or lime juice, as needed

2 cups grated raw beets

1 avocado, peeled, pitted, and smashed with a fork

1 cup sprouts, such as pea sprouts or broccoli sprouts

To make the spread, in the bowl of a food processor or blender, combine the carrots, ginger, shallot, miso, honey, and vinegar and process until fairly smooth, 1 to 2 minutes. It will still have a somewhat chunky texture from the carrots. With the motor running, drizzle in the sesame oil and salt and process until thoroughly combined. Set aside.

Cut the white stalk from the end of the collard green leaves and discard. Rinse the leaves with warm water to bring them to room temperature. Lay them on a dish towel and use a paring knife to shave down the stalk, making it the same thickness as the rest of the leaf. This will make it easier to roll.

In a bowl, stir together the cooked quinoa and tahini, adding a bit of lemon juice if necessary so that the ingredients are evenly distributed. On your work surface, arrange two of the collard green leaves head to foot, overlapping them halfway and creating a circular shape (this gives you more surface area). Spread a generous amount of the miso-carrot spread down the middle, then layer a quarter each of the quinoa, beets, avocado, and sprouts onto the leaves. Fold over each end, tuck one side under, and roll like a burrito. Serve immediately, or wrap in plastic wrap and store in the fridge for up to 2 days.

I remember the first time I went to the farmers' market at the San Francisco Ferry Building, a gigantic place with the largest variety of gorgeous vegetables I've ever seen. There was a vegan booth that sold fresh juices in mason jars and a few different veggie wraps filled with a variety of spreads and vegetables, which were my inspiration for this recipe. At first glance it looks like a bunch of hippie mush, but it actually delivers layers of flavors and crunch. The collard green leaves are hearty and crisp, while the insides are soft and full of flavor from the carrot miso spread. I am aware this kind of vegan snack isn't for everyone, but it gives you a burst of energy, can be wrapped up and taken on the go, and makes you feel good about your lunch. There is a time to splurge and a time to feed your body goodness, and this wrap, a healthy burrito of sorts, makes up for some of the former.

lemon and herb hummus

SERVES 6 TO 8 <

3 cups cooked chickpeas (about two 15-ounce cans)

1 roasted shallot (see note)

3 tablespoons tahini

Grated zest and juice of 1 lemon

Sea salt and freshly ground pepper

Pinch of red pepper flakes

1/3 cup extra-virgin olive oil

3 tablespoons chopped fresh flat-leaf parsley

3 tablespoons chopped fresh dill, plus extra for garnish

3 tablespoons chopped fresh basil leaves

OPTIONAL GARNISH

1/2 English cucumber, sliced paper-thin

2 teaspoons finely chopped fresh flat-leaf parsley, plus extra for garnish

1 tablespoon champagne vinegar

1/3 cup crumbled feta cheese

In a food processor, combine the chickpeas, roasted shallot, tahini, lemon zest and juice, 1 teaspoon salt, 1 teaspoon pepper, and the red pepper flakes and pulse to combine. With the motor running, pour in the olive oil in a steady stream. Stop the food processor when the hummus reaches the desired smoothness (I like mine a bit textured). Add the herbs to the hummus, and pulse a few times until combined. Taste and add more salt and pepper, if you'd like. Pulse the processor while adding 1 to 3 tablespoons water to thin out the hummus as needed, remembering that it will firm up in the fridge.

To make the optional garnish, toss the cucumber with the parsley and vinegar. To serve, put the hummus on a serving plate, top with the cucumber mixture and feta, and garnish with fresh chopped parsley and dill.

To roast the shallot, peel it and cut into quarters. Rub a bit of olive oil on the surface and roast in the oven or a toaster oven at 400°F for about 20 minutes.

I would be lying if I told you I always made my own hummus. I like the flavor of homemade hummus, and it's so much fresher than store-bought, but I go through the stuff too quickly to keep up. If you have a food processor pretty much all you have to do is dump and blend, but it can be made in a blender as well.

I've dressed up this version just a bit with an optional cucumber salad on top, which makes it presentable for guests or perfect for taking over to a friend's house. If you're short on time, you can omit the roasted shallot and use 2 cloves of raw garlic instead.

crunchy curried chickpeas

SERVES 4 TO 6 <

3 1/4 cups cooked chickpeas (about two 15-ounce cans)

2 tablespoons extra-virgin olive oil

2 teaspoons sweet curry powder

1/2 teaspoon dried thyme

1 teaspoon fresh grated ginger

Sea salt or garlic salt

Preheat the oven to 400°F.

Rinse the chickpeas and drain completely. Lay them on a dish towel and gently rub them to remove any remaining skins, making sure that they are totally dry. In a large bowl, stir together the olive oil, curry powder, thyme, and ginger. Add the chickpeas to the bowl and toss to coat. Spread the chickpeas on a parchment-lined rimmed baking sheet.

Bake the chickpeas, tossing them occasionally, until they are light brown and crisped, 40 to 45 minutes. As soon as you remove them from the oven, sprinkle with a teaspoon of salt. Taste and add more salt if you like. Let them cool completely (this will make them crunchier), then serve. These are best eaten the day they are made.

These are the perfect bar snack—small, salty, and crunchy. I will warn you that they are a bit finicky, and it's not always easy achieving the perfect crunch. But if you make sure to drain the chickpeas well, don't get too heavy-handed with the oil, and let them cool before serving, you'll end up with an addictive snack. They also make a nice alternative to croutons in a salad, bringing a bit of crunch to the bowl.

beach day tuna salad

SERVES 2 <

2 (5-ounce) cans water-packed tuna

1/4 cup golden raisins

2 celery stalks, diced

2 tablespoons finely chopped fresh
    flat-leaf parsley

2 tablespoons whole grain mustard

2 tablespoons freshly squeezed
    lemon juice

2 tablespoons extra-virgin olive oil or
    good-quality mayonnaise

Sea salt and freshly ground pepper

Sturdy whole grain crackers, for
    dipping

Drain the tuna and put it in a mixing bowl. Soak the raisins in warm water for 5 minutes to soften, then drain. Coarsely chop the raisins and add them to the tuna. Add the celery, parsley, mustard, lemon juice, and olive oil or mayonnaise to the bowl and stir well to combine. Add salt and pepper to taste.

Serve at once with the crackers for dipping, or store, covered, in the fridge for up to 6 days.

My family pokes fun at my mom that we can count on one hand the variety of meals she made as we grew up. It's all done with love, as we were never hungry, but her interest in gardening and socializing took precedence over spending time in the kitchen. We always lived near the ocean, and summer weekends were spent at the beach with a large cooler filled with cut fruit, Capri Sun juice boxes, and my mom's tuna salad with Ritz crackers. Those days it was just mayo, mustard, and relish with canned tuna, but I have chosen to update this classic. Getting its crunch from the celery and a bit of sweetness from the golden raisins, it's a little something different. I prefer olive oil to mayonnaise here, but I included both as an option, as both taste great.

If you are not much for tuna, the salad works equally well with either shredded chicken or chickpeas as your protein. I like to use a sturdy whole grain cracker for dipping into the tuna, but you could just as well put it in a sandwich or pita bread.

honey almond butter

MAKES 1¹/₂ CUPS <

2 cups raw almonds

1 teaspoon oil, such as almond,
  unrefined peanut, or extra-virgin
  coconut

Sea salt

1¹/₂ teaspoons ground cinnamon

2 tablespoons honey

Put the almonds in a food processor or Vitamix and process for
about 1 minute. Add the oil, ¹/₄ teaspoon of salt, and the cinnamon.
Continue to process for another 8 to 10 minutes, scraping down
the sides of the food processor or Vitamix as needed. You will see a
change in consistency from crumbs, to big clumps, to a large ball.
Finally, as the oil is released from the almonds, the mixture will
smooth itself out. If you want it even smoother, add a bit more oil.

When it is as smooth as you'd like it, stir in the honey, add more salt to
taste, and transfer to a glass jar. It will keep, covered, in the fridge for
up to 6 weeks.

If you prefer a toasty flavor, roast the nuts on a baking
sheet for 10 minutes at 350°F. Let cool completely before
continuing.

This barely sweet and
mildly spiced nut butter dresses up
sliced apples, oatmeal, or a piece of
toast, or it just serves as a tasty spoonful of something when you pass by the
fridge. A food processor or Vitamix is
essential here. The nuts need to be
agitated for quite some time before
their oils come out, so don't be surprised when you see a crumbly nut
meal; just keep processing. The honey
will definitely cause the almond butter
to seize up if you add it while the nuts
are being ground, which is why it is
stirred in at the end.

Experiment using different nuts,
warm spices, or maybe even some
cocoa powder. Note that each type of
nut has a different oil content, so you
may need to adjust the amount of oil
added to get the right consistency.

toasty nuts

MAKES ABOUT 2¹/₂ CUPS <

1 egg white

2¹/₂ tablespoons Grade B maple syrup

¹/₄ to ¹/₂ teaspoon cayenne pepper

¹/₂ teaspoon freshly ground black pepper

1 teaspoon sea salt

2¹/₂ cups raw unsalted nuts mix, such as almonds, cashews, pecans, and walnuts

2 tablespoons flaxseeds

3 tablespoons millet or quinoa

1¹/₂ tablespoons finely chopped fresh rosemary

Preheat the oven to 300°F and line a rimmed baking sheet with parchment paper.

In a large mixing bowl, whisk the egg white until frothy. Whisk in the maple syrup, cayenne, black pepper, and salt. Stir in the nuts, flaxseeds, millet, and rosemary, making sure everything is coated completely.

Spread the nuts on the prepared baking sheet in an even layer and bake until the nuts are browned and fragrant, 25 to 30 minutes. Remove from the oven and let cool before serving.

Toasty nuts are a perfectly portable snack. This recipe can be adapted according to your taste, as it doesn't veer too far to either side of the sweet-to-savory spectrum. You could add in a bit of turbinado sugar if you like things sweeter, or a teaspoon of red pepper flakes if you like things extra-hot.

sesame date yogurt cups

SERVES 4 <

7 Medjool dates, pitted

2 tablespoons toasted sesame seeds, plus more for sprinkling

Sea salt

2 cups Greek or plain goat's milk yogurt

1/2 teaspoon ground cinnamon

1/2 cup crisped brown rice

Soak the dates in warm water for 10 minutes to soften. Drain and chop into pieces. Put them in a bowl with the sesame seeds and a pinch of salt and mash it all together to create a chunky paste. Press a fourth of the date mixture into the bottom of each of four small glass jars.

In a bowl, stir together the yogurt and cinnamon, then spoon 1/2 cup of the yogurt into each jar, on top of the date mixture. Sprinkle a few sesame seeds on top and add a couple spoonfuls of crisped brown rice for crunch. Enjoy cold.

I remember as a kid eating fruit-flavored yogurt that came with all that sugary jam at the bottom of the cup. Although you can still buy yogurt that way, you can naturally sweeten plain yogurt at home to make something that is both tastier and better for you. You could make these in advance to have on hand as an afternoon snack (they'll last at least a week), or increase the amount of yogurt a bit and eat it as breakfast on the go. Just leave out the crisped rice until you're ready to eat it, or it'll get soggy.

Good Medjool dates should be plenty soft enough to mash up with a knife. However, letting them sit in hot water, then draining them well, makes this step a bit easier.

strawberry and leek quesadilla

SERVES 1 <

1 leek

2 teaspoons coconut oil or extra-virgin olive oil

Sea salt and freshly ground pepper

2 brown rice tortillas

About 1/3 cup fresh goat cheese

About 1/3 cup shredded mozzarella

About 1/2 cup thinly sliced strawberries

Chopped fresh cilantro, for garnish (optional)

Trim the leek, discarding the tough green top, halve vertically, and rinse in cold water, making sure to clean out any dirt trapped between the layers. Slice into thin half circles. In a medium sauté pan, heat 1 teaspoon of the oil over medium heat. Add the leeks and a pinch of salt and sauté until completely softened and browning in spots, about 10 minutes. Transfer the leeks to a bowl and set aside.

Heat 1/2 teaspoon of the oil over medium-high heat in the sauté pan and place one of the tortillas in the pan. Sprinkle the goat cheese, mozzarella, sautéed leeks, strawberries, and a generous amount of pepper evenly over the tortilla, adjusting the quantities of each ingredient according to your taste. Cover with the second tortilla and cook until just browned on the bottom, about 2 minutes. Brush the remaining 1/2 teaspoon of oil on the top tortilla, flip, and cook until the second side is lightly browned, about 2 minutes more.

Sprinkle the quesadilla with the cilantro, if using, slice into wedges, and enjoy warm.

I posted this recipe on our blog a while back and received comments from quite a few skeptics who thought the flavor combination sounded off. I started to second-guess myself. I thought that maybe this is a combination that only I could appreciate, like putting hummus on my scrambled eggs? To date, however, it is one of the recipes for which I have received the most positive feedback after people tried it.

If you can get your hands on brown rice tortillas, I recommend them here even if you don't ordinarily buy them. When heated, these tortillas pack more of a crunch than standard tortillas, making them a nice contrast to the soft filling.

low-yolk egg salad

SERVES 2 <

5 eggs
1 celery stalk
1 tablespoon whole-milk Greek yogurt
2 teaspoons mustard

Scant 1/4 cup finely chopped fresh
chives
Sea salt and freshly ground pepper

Put the eggs in a saucepan and just cover with water. Bring the water to a gentle boil and boil for 3 minutes. Turn off the heat, cover the saucepan, and let the eggs sit in the hot water for 18 minutes. Prepare a bowl of water with ice in it. Drain the eggs and immediately transfer them to the ice bath.

While the eggs cool, finely dice the celery. Combine the celery, yogurt, mustard, and chives in a mixing bowl. Once the eggs are cool, remove the shells. Discard 3 of the yolks and finely dice the remaining two whole eggs and three whites. Add the eggs to the bowl and stir everything until thoroughly combined. Add a few pinches of salt and pepper to taste. Serve immediately or keep covered in the fridge for up to 4 days.

There are a number of great nutrients in an egg yolk, but those who are watching their weight or their cholesterol might want to try this egg salad, which is a bit lighter than the traditional version. You could certainly throw in all of the egg yolks if you please, but I like how this salad has a lighter mouthfeel as opposed to the density of the yolk and mayonnaise in traditional egg salad. Don't let me deter you from the mayonnaise either; it's an easy replacement for the yogurt I've used here. This egg salad, which is heavy on the chives and has just enough yogurt and mustard to hold it all together, is perfect atop a piece of toasted whole grain bread.

I don't specify the type of mustard here, since everyone has their own favorite. I use Dijon, but a hot mustard with a bit of horseradish would be interesting in here too.

granola protein bars

MAKES 8 LARGE BARS <

1¹/₄ cups old-fashioned rolled oats

¹/₂ cup slivered almonds

¹/₂ cup coarsely chopped raw cashews

¹/₂ cup brown rice syrup

1 tablespoon water

1 teaspoon pure vanilla extract

1 teaspoon ground cinnamon

¹/₄ teaspoon sea salt

1 cup crisp brown rice cereal

¹/₂ cup vanilla protein powder

1 cup dried cherries, chopped

Preheat the oven to 350°F. Spread the oats, almonds, and cashews on a rimmed baking sheet and bake until just barely toasted, about 10 minutes. Remove from the oven and let cool.

Turn the heat down to 300°F. In a large mixing bowl, stir together the brown rice syrup, water, vanilla, cinnamon, and salt. Add the toasted oats and nuts, the rice cereal, and protein powder and stir until everything is coated. Stir in the cherries.

Line an 8 by 8-inch baking pan with parchment paper, leaving an overhang on two sides for easy removal. Dump the granola mixture in the center. Using a large spoon or your fingers, press the mixture down compactly (wetting the spoon or your fingers with warm water when they get sticky will help), being sure to push it all the way to the corners. Bake until the top is slightly toasted, 23 to 25 minutes.

Remove from the oven and let cool completely. Pull them out by the parchment edges and cut eight bars of equal size.

If you're going to eat them later, wrap each bar individually in plastic wrap. They should keep fresh for about a week.

These bars have served me well on many long drives, are ideal for taking on a day hike, and make a compact airplane snack. They are perfectly chewy, with a bit of crunch from the crisp rice and nuts.

I chose a variety of nuts and grains for texture and variety, but you could streamline this recipe a bit for a shorter grocery list. Think ratios: you could use 2¹/₂ cups of oats or crisped rice instead of using both, and you could try 1 cup of either almonds or cashews if you don't have both. Honey will work as an alternative sweetener, though the resulting bars will be tackier than if you use the brown rice syrup.

coconut loaf

SERVES 6 TO 8 <

1/4 cup extra-virgin coconut oil, melted, plus more for the pan

2 cups unsweetened shredded coconut

3/4 cup turbinado sugar

3/4 cup unbleached all-purpose flour

1 cup whole wheat pastry flour

1/2 teaspoon freshly grated nutmeg

11/2 teaspoons baking powder

1/2 teaspoon baking soda

1/2 teaspoon sea salt

2 eggs

1 (13.5-ounce) can coconut milk

1 teaspoon pure vanilla extract

1 cup organic powdered sugar, or more as needed

2 cups fresh blackberries

Preheat the oven to 350°F. Grease an 8 1/2-inch loaf pan with a thin coat of coconut oil.

Spread the shredded coconut on a rimmed baking sheet and toast in the oven until just golden brown, about 4 minutes. Watch it carefully, as it can burn very quickly. Set aside 1/2 cup for topping the loaf.

In a large mixing bowl, combine 1 1/2 cups of the toasted coconut and the turbinado sugar. Sift in the flours, nutmeg, baking powder, baking soda, and salt and stir to combine. In another bowl, whisk the eggs together, then whisk in 1 cup of the coconut milk, the coconut oil, and the vanilla. Gently stir the wet mixture into the dry ingredients until just combined. Pour the mixture into the loaf pan and bake until a toothpick inserted in the middle comes out clean, 45 to 50 minutes. Remove from the oven and let cool to room temperature.

While the loaf is cooling, combine 1/4 cup of the remaining coconut milk and the powdered sugar in a bowl and whisk until there are no clumps. Add more sugar or more coconut milk to taste, depending on the consistency you prefer. (You won't use the entire can of coconut milk.) Pour the glaze over the cooled cake and sprinkle the remaining toasted coconut on top. Cut into slices. Toast each slice, if you like. Serve with a handful of fresh blackberries.

The coconut flavor of this loaf is pretty subtle, even though it contains three different coconut-based ingredients. Fresh out of the oven, it is fairly crumbly. As it rests, it holds together better, and a slice will stand up well to a few minutes in the toaster oven before you garnish it. Hugh believes you really must have a sweet to go with your coffee, so it's nice to have this loaf around that can pass for a breakfast pastry or after-noon snack. You can also dress it up for dessert with a bit of fresh whipping cream or ice cream.

If all you can find is sweetened shred-ded coconut (it's easier to come by than the unsweetened variety), simply scale back the turbinado sugar by about 2 tablespoons. The loaf can be made a day in advance and kept cov-ered until serving. If you're serving a group, you can arrange the slices on a baking sheet and put them under the broiler for a minute or two to warm them through and toast the edges before adding the berries.

zucchini bread bites

MAKES 2 DOZEN <

1 egg

1/2 teaspoon pure vanilla extract

3 tablespoons extra-virgin olive oil

1/2 cup maple syrup

3/4 cup quinoa flakes

3/4 cup oat flour

1/2 teaspoon baking soda

1/4 teaspoon baking powder

2 tablespoons natural (nonalkalized) cocoa powder

1/2 teaspoon ground cinnamon

1/2 teaspoon sea salt

1/4 cup plus 1 1/2 tablespoons turbinado sugar

3/4 cup finely grated zucchini

1/2 cup chopped lightly toasted walnuts

In a bowl, whisk together the egg, vanilla, olive oil, and maple syrup. In another bowl, stir together the quinoa flakes, oat flour, baking soda, baking powder, cocoa powder, cinnamon, salt, and 1/4 cup of the turbinado sugar, breaking up any clumps.

Squeeze the excess water from the shredded zucchini in a cheesecloth or with your hands, break it up, and stir into the wet ingredients. Add the wet ingredients to the dry and stir to combine. Stir in the walnuts. The batter will be pretty moist. Cover and refrigerate for 30 minutes.

While the batter is resting, arrange a rack in the upper third of your oven and preheat the oven to 375°F.

Line a baking sheet with parchment paper or a nonstick silicone baking mat. Using your hands, gently roll a heaping tablespoonful of the dough into a ball and place it on the baking sheet. Repeat with the remaining batter, spreading the balls evenly on the baking sheet. Gently flatten the top of each ball and sprinkle the tops with the remaining 1 1/2 tablespoons of turbinado sugar. Bake, rotating the pan halfway through the baking time, until the edges are browned and you can push on the top of one with a soft resistance, 12 to 14 minutes. Allow to cool completely before serving. Stored in an airtight container, they will keep 2 to 3 days in the refrigerator.

This great gluten-free snack—softer than a cookie but firmer than a muffin—reminds me of a bite of tender zucchini bread. Since we're talking snacks here, not treats, they are not too sweet. You could always stir in some dark chocolate chips or make a quick cream cheese glaze if you want something more decadent.

I find quinoa flakes in health food stores or in well-stocked grocery stores next to the oatmeal. It is often used as a breakfast porridge, but here it replaces the flour to create a very light texture. If you can't find it, you could double the amount of oat flour, or you could substitute 1 cup of cooked and cooled quinoa.

There are two types of unsweetened cocoa powder: natural (nonalkalized) and Dutch process. The natural, non-alkalized type is merely roasted cocoa beans that are ground into a fine powder. It has a slight bitterness to it and a deeper flavor than Dutch process cocoa, and it will react with baking soda to leaven a baked good. Dutch process, or alkalized, cocoa powder has a mellower chocolate flavor, and because its acids have been neutralized, it doesn't react with baking soda and is more often used with baking powder. You can use them interchangeably, if you adjust your use of baking soda or powder accordingly, but I like to use natural cocoa powder.

nut and seed crackers

MAKES ABOUT 24 CRACKERS <

1/2 cup almond meal

1/2 cup raw cashews

2 tablespoons ground flaxseed (flax meal)

1/3 cup sesame seeds

2 tablespoons fresh thyme leaves

3/4 teaspoon sea salt

1 tablespoon maple syrup

1 tablespoon extra-virgin coconut oil

1 to 2 tablespoons water, as needed

Combine the almond meal, cashews, and ground flaxseed in a food processor and pulse a few times just until evenly ground. Add the sesame seeds, thyme, 1/2 teaspoon of the salt, the maple syrup, and coconut oil and pulse a few more times. Add the water, 1 tablespoon at a time, until the mixture just begins to stick together. Form the dough into a ball, wrap in plastic wrap, and chill for at least 1 hour or up to overnight.

Preheat the oven to 325°F and line a rimmed baking sheet with parchment paper.

Remove the dough from the fridge, put it between two sheets of parchment paper, and roll it out to 1/8-inch thickness. You want it to be thin, but if it's too thin you won't be able to pick up the finished crackers without breaking them. Using a sharp knife, cut the crackers into the shape of your choice. Using a sharp-edged spatula to get under the cracker pieces, gently place the crackers on the prepared baking sheet with 1/4-inch space between them. Bake the crackers, rotating the baking sheet halfway through the cooking time, until the edges look toasted, 11 to 13 minutes. Sprinkle the remaining 1/4 teaspoon of salt on top and let cool completely before serving.

I keep hummus in my fridge at all times. Some would consider it a dip, but I consider it a staple condiment, like ketchup or soy sauce. I put it on all sorts of things, but these crackers and hummus are the perfect pair. The delicate dough needs to be chilled, which takes some time, but these homemade crackers are something special.

nori popcorn

1 tablespoon toasted sesame oil

1 tablespoon coconut oil or other
    neutral oil

1/3 cup popcorn kernels

2 tablespoons natural cane sugar

2 tablespoons toasted sesame seeds

1/2 teaspoon sea salt

Freshly ground pepper

5 sheets roasted nori (seaweed snack),
    crumbled

Low-sodium soy sauce, in a spray
    bottle (optional)

In a large pot with a lid, heat the sesame and coconut oils over high
heat. Add the popcorn kernels and stir. Once you hear the kernels
start to sizzle, add the sugar and sesame seeds, shake, and cover with
the lid. Continue to shake vigorously over the heat while the popcorn
pops, 2 to 3 minutes.

Once you hear the popping slow, transfer the popcorn to a rimmed
baking sheet and sprinkle with the salt, a few grinds of pepper, and
the nori. Toss to mix. Because there is not a ton of sugar in this recipe,
the nori and sesame seeds won't adhere to the popcorn too well. If
you like, you can make them stick to the popcorn better by misting
the popcorn with a few sprays of soy sauce and tossing to mix
everything once more.

The popcorn is best eaten immediately, but it can be stored in an
airtight container for a few hours before serving.

**I usually prefer sweet
snacks** to salty ones, but popcorn
is just too easy to make, not to mention mesmerizing as it flies around
under the lid of the pot. There were
a few months when *Food & Wine*
magazine published a couple different popcorn recipes that intrigued
me. My version, which is inspired by
one of theirs, is a light snack to get
you through the afternoon lull. The
sesame oil just hints at its flavor, while
a bit of sugar gives the sesame seeds
and salt something to stick to. The
roasted nori, once it is all crumbled
up, gets hidden in the crannies of
the popcorn, where it adds its subtle
flavor. Kids actually love the dried
seaweed; I find that adults tend to be
more particular about the taste. These
days nori is easy to find at both regular
markets and health food stores. If you
like things with a bit of heat, sift a very
light sprinkle of wasabi powder on top
of the finished popcorn, or use wasabi
nori if you come across it.

greens smoothie

SERVES 2 <

2 kale leaves, stemmed and chopped

1 cup almond milk, or more as needed

Big handful baby spinach

1 frozen ripe banana

1 pear or apple, sliced

Handful of crushed ice

Combine the kale, almond milk, spinach, banana, pear, crushed ice, and a splash of water in a powerful blender and puree until everything is completely smooth. Add more almond milk, if you like, to achieve the consistency you prefer. Serve immediately.

Although an all-fruit smoothie makes a nice snack, throwing some dark leafy greens in there adds a nice nutrition boost without taking away from the sweetness. You won't even taste the greens as long as you're using sweet, ripe fruit. When you have bananas that are on their last leg, chop them into big chunks and freeze them so you'll always have on hand frozen bananas, which give this shake its creaminess. If you prefer a sweeter drink, add a chopped pitted date to the blender.

5

The Happy Hour

When Hugh and I get together with our friends, it's less often for dinner parties and more frequently for drinks and appetizers. It's an easy way for everyone to contribute and to have a variety of nibbles while we all catch up on life's happenings. There are cooler, darker evenings when a warm spinach and artichoke dip is called for, and backyard parties where mango guacamole is the simplest way to feed a group. Maybe you want to serve something more elaborate, like the beets and greens, but in any case you'll find something in this chapter fit for any occasion with friends, even if it's just a cocktail.

white sangria

SERVES 4 <

1 (750-ml) bottle viognier or
    sauvignon blanc

1 nectarine, pitted and sliced

1 orange, thinly sliced

$1/4$ cup orange liqueur, such as
    Cointreau

1 cup fresh blackberries

1 cup sparkling lemonade or ginger ale

Handful of fresh mint leaves

Place 4 highball glasses in the freezer to chill.

In a large pitcher, combine the wine, nectarine, orange, and
Cointreau. Cover and let sit in the fridge for at least 1 hour and up
to 6 hours. When ready to serve, stir in the blackberries, sparkling
lemonade, and mint leaves.

Serve cold in the chilled glasses.

My girlfriends and I are
all wine drinkers. We're not exactly
picky, but it's the beverage of choice
when we get together and catch up.
Although we have fun trying different
bottles, you can't beat a pretty pitcher
of sangria with fresh fruit floating
around. It is easy to make and tough to
mess up, so whether you're hosting a
dinner party or just getting together to
chat with friends, this is a great drink
to try.

Although a number of sangria recipes call for simple syrup (made from
equal parts sugar and water), I find
that between the fruit and sparkling
beverage, you get all the sweetness
you need. Both lemonade and ginger
ale are welcome here, though they
impart a different flavor. I'm guessing
that you're already partial to one or
the other. By adding the blackberries
at the end, it keeps them from bleed-
ing into the sangria and changing the
drink's color.

black cherry refresher

SERVES 6 <

12 cherries, pitted

Roughly 2 tablespoons fresh mint leaves, plus more for garnish

1 cup gin

1/4 cup St. Germain Elderflower Liqueur

1 cup cherry juice

Ice

11/4 cups sparkling water, or as needed

6 lime wedges, for garnish

In the bottom of a glass pitcher, using a muddler, muddle the cherries and mint together until the mint is crushed and the cherries release some of their juice. Add the gin, elderflower liqueur, and cherry juice and stir to combine.

To serve, fill 6 highball glasses with ice, divide the cherry mixture evenly among the glasses, and top each with sparkling water (the amount needed will vary depending on the size of your glasses). Garnish each glass with a lime wedge and serve immediately. Or, if you prefer, combine the cherry mixture and sparkling water in a pitcher, put a bowl of lime wedges and an ice bucket alongside, and let your guests serve themselves.

My mom may not be much of a cook, but she is renowned among our family and friends for her cocktail-making skills. I was lucky to have her as a sounding board when I was writing these drink recipes, as I'm pretty sure my fun-loving mom came out of the womb with a cocktail glass in her hand.

I know that many mixologists specify precise measurements, but I bring my philosophy about cooking to the bar as well and suggest that you taste as you go along and tweak the quantities as you desire. Neither too strong nor sickeningly sweet, this is the perfect daytime cocktail, suitable for a brunch or a wedding shower. For those who don't like the herbal flavor of gin, vodka is a nice alternative. You'll want to use 100 percent cherry juice, with no sugar or anything else added, to get that perfectly tart flavor.

grapefruit margarita

SERVES 1 <

Turbinado sugar, for the rim

4 segments pink grapefruit, membrane removed (see page 54)

Ice

$1/4$ cup (2 ounces) freshly squeezed grapefruit juice

1 tablespoon ($1/2$ ounce) agave nectar, as needed

2 tablespoons (1 ounce) triple sec

$1/4$ cup (2 ounces) reposado tequila

Splash of coconut water

Pour a thin layer of the sugar onto a small plate. Rub a wedge of grapefruit around the rim of an old-fashioned-size glass, and roll the rim in the plate of sugar to coat. Set aside.

Put the grapefruit segments at the bottom of the prepared glass and fill it with ice. Add the grapefruit juice, agave nectar, triple sec, and tequila and give it a quick stir. Top the drink off with a generous splash of coconut water. Serve immediately.

You'll have to use your discretion

when making this recipe. I have tasted a few grapefruits whose juice is plenty sweet for this drink, but if yours is more tart, you'll want to include the agave nectar. Squeezing citrus juice is pretty straightforward, but if you prefer, you can find fresh-squeezed grapefruit juice at well-stocked markets. Coconut water, trendy beverage it is, doesn't taste particularly like coconut nor is it very sweet, but it adds a nice subtle twist to the margarita. Here I give the measurements for making one margarita, but you can multiply the quantities as needed and mix everything in a pitcher.

cucumber crush

SERVES 4 <

1 cucumber

About 2 tablespoons loosely packed
    tarragon leaves

Juice of 1 large lime

$3/4$ cup vodka

$1/4$ cup agave nectar

Crushed ice for serving

1 cup sparkling water

Cut eight thin slices from the cucumber and set aside for garnish. If you have a juicer, use it to juice the cucumber. If you don't, cut the cucumber in half lengthwise, scoop out the seeds and discard, and coarsely chop the flesh. Place the cucumber pieces in a food processor or blender and puree for about 1 minute. Pour into a fine-mesh sieve set over a bowl, pressing the solids to release as much juice as possible. This should yield a scant cup of cucumber juice.

Coarsely chop the tarragon leaves a few times to release their oils. In a small pitcher, combine the cucumber juice, tarragon, lime juice, vodka, and agave nectar. Stir to combine.

To serve, fill four old-fashioned-size glasses with crushed ice. Divide the mixture among the glasses and top off with the sparkling water. Garnish each glass with two of the reserved cucumber slices.

A number of my kitchen experiments

are inspired by an excess of a certain ingredient. In this case, I had a crisper drawer full of cucumbers from my CSA basket, and it was time to start juicing. Strained cucumber juice and sparkling water is a refreshing drink for a warm day, but it also makes a crisp cocktail, here sweetened with agave nectar, which dissolves in liquid much like simple syrup.

The directions below instruct you how to make a small pitcher, since I don't want you to be fussing over every cocktail individually. The recipe can easily be multiplied for a crowd; just leave the sparkling water on the side to add to each drink as you serve it, as it will go flat sitting in the pitcher for too long. If you'd like a less potent drink or you don't want to be able to taste the vodka, scale the vodka back to $1/2$ cup or add a bit more sparkling water to top off the glass.

baked artichoke dip

SERVES 6 TO 8 <

5 cups fresh baby spinach (about 15 ounces)

1 1/2 cups cannellini beans (one 15-ounce can)

1 cup jarred or canned artichoke hearts

2 cloves garlic

1/2 teaspoon red pepper flakes

1 teaspoon dried oregano

1 teaspoon sea salt

Small handful of fresh flat-leaf parsley leaves, plus more for garnish

3 tablespoons extra-virgin olive oil, plus more for the dish

Grated zest of 1 lemon

1 tablespoon fresh lemon juice

1/2 cup freshly grated Parmesan cheese

1 cup shredded mozzarella

Crudités, sliced bread, or crackers, for dipping

In this lighter take on a typically heavy classic, creamy white beans add a hearty, almost hummus-like consistency to the dip. Of course there is also cheese. There *has* to be melted cheese in artichoke dip.

One packed cup of thawed and drained frozen spinach can be substituted for the fresh, though I prefer the color of fresh spinach, and the long pieces of spinach that are strewn through the dish. This can easily be made a day in advance and kept in the fridge until ready to bake. I've also found the leftovers make a really nice sandwich spread as well.

Preheat the oven to 400°F.

In a large pot with a steamer insert, steam the spinach until just wilted, 1 to 2 minutes. Transfer to a colander to drain. When it's cool enough to touch, squeeze out the water with your hands and coarsely chop. Set aside.

Drain the beans and artichoke hearts. Combine the garlic, red pepper flakes, oregano, salt, and parsley in a food processor and pulse to coarsely chop. Add the beans, artichoke hearts, olive oil, lemon zest, and juice to the processor and give it a few pulses until it forms a chunky puree. Transfer the mixture to a bowl.

In a separate bowl, stir together the Parmesan and mozzarella. Add half of the cheese mixture and all of the spinach to the bean mixture, stirring with a spoon to break up any clumps.

Grease an ovenproof dish such as an 8-inch cast-iron pan. Pour the dip into the pan and sprinkle the remaining cheese mixture on top. Bake until just browned and bubbly, 15 to 20 minutes. Garnish the dip with some chopped parsley and serve hot with the crudités or bread.

polenta squares with raw corn and blueberry relish

SERVES 6 <

3/4 cup whole milk or nut milk, such as almond milk

1 clove garlic, minced

1 cup water

3/4 cup polenta

1/2 teaspoon dried Mexican oregano

Sea salt and freshly ground pepper

1/4 cup freshly grated Parmesan cheese

2 ears of corn

1 1/4 cups blueberries

2 tablespoons finely chopped fresh oregano or fresh cilantro

2 teaspoons rice wine vinegar

2 teaspoons extra-virgin olive oil, plus more for the pan

1 jalapeño chile, stemmed, seeded, and diced

Preheat the oven to 425°F. Lightly oil an 8-inch-square glass or ceramic baking dish.

In a saucepan, combine the milk, garlic, and water and bring to a boil over medium-high heat. Add the polenta and dried oregano, turn the heat to low, and cook, stirring occasionally, until the polenta is thick and has lost its grittiness, about 10 minutes. Season generously with salt and pepper and stir in the Parmesan. Pour the polenta into the prepared baking dish and bake until the top is golden brown, 40 to 45 minutes. Set aside to cool.

Using a sharp knife, cut the kernels from both corn cobs and put the kernels in a mixing bowl. Cut half of the blueberries in half, leaving the rest intact. Add the blueberries to the corn along with the fresh oregano, rice vinegar, olive oil, jalapeño, and a pinch or two of salt and stir to combine.

Cut the cooled polenta into nine squares and serve with the corn mixture on the side, or top each square with a heaping spoonful of the corn mixture and serve.

This recipe's corn and blueberry topping was quite popular at all of our get-togethers last summer. I started out serving it on polenta squares, as described below, but then I found I could save myself some time by serving the salsa-like topping with some corn chips. The recipe then morphed into a salad when I tossed the corn and blueberries with some tender greens and a bit of queso fresco. I even used it as a topping for grilled white fish. With its fresh kernels of crisp corn and sweet, juicy berries, this versatile combination is not to be missed in the thick of summer, when both of these items are at their peak. The corn is used raw here, so find the freshest cobs you can. The heat of the jalapeño is in the seeds. You can scrape them all out if you want very little heat, leave a few in for mild heat, and go from there.

grilled zucchini roll-ups

MAKES 20 TO 24 ROLL-UPS <

ZA'ATAR
1/4 cup toasted sesame seeds
1/4 cup dried sumac
3 tablespoons dried thyme
1 tablespoon dried oregano

ROLL-UPS
5 medium zucchini
Sea salt and freshly ground pepper
1/2 cup whole-milk Greek yogurt
3 tablespoons tahini
1 tablespoon extra-virgin olive oil
1 to 2 tablespoons fresh thyme leaves
Toasted sesame seeds, for garnish

To make the za'atar, in a bowl, stir together the sesame seeds, sumac, thyme, and oregano. Set aside.

To make the roll-ups, cut the ends from the zucchini and slice in strips lengthwise, about 1/8 inch thick. Save the end strips, with rounded edges, for another use. Rub a few pinches of salt into the zucchini flesh.

In a bowl, stir together the yogurt, tahini and a pinch of salt and set aside.

Heat your grill or grill pan to medium-high. Lay the zucchini on a baking sheet, brush lightly with the olive oil, and add a few grinds of pepper. Grill, turning once, until just softened, about 2 minutes per side. Return the zucchini slices to the baking sheet.

Once the zucchini slices have cooled slightly, swipe about 1 table-spoon of the yogurt mixture lengthwise down the middle of a zucchini slice and generously sprinkle some za'atar on top, about a scant 1/2 teaspoon per roll-up. (You'll have lots of za'atar left over. Save it for another use, like sprinkling it on top of hummus.) Add a pinch of fresh thyme leaves and, starting from one of the narrow ends, roll the zucchini into a roll. Garnish with a few sesame seeds and serve at room temperature.

With the exception of crudités or a Mediterranean dip, I am guilty of including cheese in most of my appetizers. These roll-ups, however, are a flavor-packed alternative. The tahini and yogurt make the zucchini perfectly creamy, and the za'atar adds a bit of bite. Made using sumac and other ingredients, za'atar is a Middle Eastern spice blend that has a ton of health benefits and also adds a pleasant acidic flavor to foods. I've described how to make your own, but most spice shops and international grocers sell it already mixed. Their versions may include fennel, coriander, or cumin, but they all will work fine here.

Thicker zucchini will produce strips that are easier to work with. If you cut them too thick, however, they won't roll up; too thin, and they turn to mush. If you have a mandoline that allows you adjust the blade to cut foods to various thicknesses, that's the most reliable option. It's perfectly fine to cut the zucchini by hand, too, as long as you pay attention to slicing them uniformly.

tempeh balls

SERVES 4 <

$^{1}/_{2}$ cup lightly toasted cashews

1 tablespoon ground flaxseed (flax meal)

2 tablespoons water

1 (8-ounce) package tempeh

2 cloves garlic

2 tablespoons extra-virgin olive oil, plus more for brushing

1 tablespoon white balsamic vinegar

$^{1}/_{2}$ cup chopped yellow onion

$^{1}/_{4}$ cup chopped fresh flat-leaf parsley, oregano, basil, or a combination

1 teaspoon fennel seeds

1 teaspoon sea salt

$1^{1}/_{2}$ cups of your favorite marinara sauce

1 teaspoon red pepper flakes

In a food processor, pulse the cashews until they form a coarse meal. Don't overprocess the nuts or you might end up with cashew butter. In a small bowl, stir together the ground flaxseed with the water to form a thin paste. Add the paste to the processor along with the cashew meal. Crumble the tempeh and add it, the garlic, olive oil, balsamic vinegar, onion, herbs, fennel seeds, and salt to the food processor. Pulse a couple times to combine; the mix should remain a bit chunky. I hate to say this in a vegan recipe, but it should resemble the texture of ground beef. Transfer the mixture to a bowl, cover, and let rest in the fridge for at least 15 minutes and up to a day in advance.

Preheat the oven to 425°F. Line a rimmed baking sheet with parchment paper.

Using your hands, gently roll the tempeh mixture into 1-inch balls and place them on the prepared baking sheet. Using a pastry brush, thinly coat the top of each ball with olive oil. Bake until the tops of the tempeh balls are just toasted, 15 to 17 minutes.

While they bake, combine the marinara sauce and red pepper flakes in a saucepan and warm over medium heat until the sauce comes to a bare simmer. When the tempeh balls are done, spear each with a cocktail pick, arrange them on a platter, and serve with the spicy marinara alongside for dipping.

Tempeh, which is originally from Indonesia, is a staple protein in several countries, as it's an inexpensive and healthful source of protein and fiber. It's meatier in texture than tofu and similar soy products, which makes it perfect for preparing these veggie "meatballs." Although I like to serve these on cocktail picks as an appetizer, they are also great in a pita sandwich or served on top of some mixed greens, especially if you pair them with some tzatziki (page 132) or lemon-tahini dressing (page 69) instead of the bright red marinara sauce suggested here.

This recipe includes ground flaxseed as a binder to keep it vegan, but you could use a whole egg as an alternative. Don't be deterred if you don't own a food processor; you can use almond meal or bread crumbs to stand in for the cashews, and everything else can be mixed by hand. They save well, kept in the fridge in an airtight container, for up to five days.

grilled eggplant pita pizzette

SERVES 6 <

1 large globe eggplant

Sea salt and freshly ground pepper

3 tablespoons extra-virgin olive oil,
  plus more for the pan

1 head roasted garlic (page 226)

3 whole grain pita breads

3/4 cup shredded smoked mozzarella
  (about 6 ounces)

1/2 cup thinly sliced red onion

1/4 cup freshly grated Parmesan

1 to 2 tablespoons za'atar (optional;
  page 177)

Coarsely chopped fresh cilantro, for
  garnish

Use a paring knife to peel the eggplant. Cut lengthwise into 1/4-inch slices. Place the slices in a colander, sprinkle with 1 teaspoon salt, and let sit for at least 30 minutes or up to an hour so that the eggplant releases some of its moisture.

Heat your grill pan over medium-high heat and rub the pan with a bit of olive oil. Wrap the eggplant pieces in a paper towel and gently press out the water the eggplant released. Working in batches as necessary, place the eggplant in the grill pan in a single layer and cook until grill marks appear on the bottom, 5 to 8 minutes, then flip and cook 5 minutes on the second side. Repeat with the remaining eggplant. Transfer the eggplant to a plate and drizzle with 1 table-spoon of the olive oil.

When the head of roasted garlic is cool enough to handle, pinch about 6 of the cloves out of their skins into a small bowl. Reserve the remaining garlic for another use. Add the remaining 2 tablespoons of olive oil and a pinch of salt and, using a fork, smash the garlic until you get a coarse paste.

Arrange a rack in the upper third of your oven and preheat the broiler. Put the pita breads on a rimmed baking sheet and spread the garlic oil on top. Sprinkle with the mozzarella, then layer with the eggplant slices and red onion. Sprinkle with the Parmesan cheese

Eggplants, those purple spheres that come in all sorts of varieties, are funny vegetables. Their flesh retains a lot of water, so I suggest letting them sit with a bit of salt, which helps them to release some of that moisture and yields a better texture in the finished dish. Although the smoked mozzarella in this recipe adds a lot of flavor, za'atar, a Middle Eastern spice blend made of sumac, dried thyme, and sesame seeds, would be a wonderful addition too. It is by no means crucial, but if you have some, a generous sprinkle will do. There are directions on page 226 for roasting a head of garlic—never a bad thing to have on hand.

I use a grill pan and oven here, but these pizzettes would also be excellent prepared on an outdoor grill, which would add even more smokiness.

and a grind of pepper. Broil until the cheese gets a few brown spots, 8 to 10 minutes. Sprinkle with za'atar as soon as you remove them from the oven.

Let the pizzette rest a few minutes to set, then garnish with fresh cilantro, cut into slices, and serve.

mediterranean baked feta

SERVES 6 <

1 (8- to 10-ounce) block of feta

1 cup assorted baby tomatoes, halved

1/3 cup kalamata olives, pitted and coarsely chopped

1/4 cup thinly sliced red onions

1 clove garlic, minced

2 tablespoons finely chopped fresh flat-leaf parsley

1 teaspoon dried oregano

1 teaspoon extra-virgin olive oil

Freshly ground pepper

Crackers, pita chips, or crostini, for dipping

Heat your grill to medium-high or preheat the oven to 400°F. Set the block of feta in the middle of a piece of parchment paper or foil for grilling, or in a small ovenproof baking dish twice the size of your block of cheese for baking.

In a bowl, mix the tomatoes, olives, onion, garlic, parsley, oregano, olive oil, and a few grinds of pepper.

Pile the tomato mixture on top of the feta. For grilling, fold up the edges of the parchment so that it will hold in any liquid as it cooks, put it straight on the grill, and heat for 15 minute to warm through. For baking, put the baking dish in the oven and bake for 15 minutes. It will not melt, just get warm and soften.

Remove from the grill or oven and serve the dip hot with the crackers, pita chips, or crostini.

This appetizer is undeniably simple, but it's far too convenient not to share with you. It reminds me of classic Greek salad components, in appetizer form. It can be brought on a camping trip and cooked over a fire, put on a hot grill while dining al fresco, or cooked in the oven and transferred to a pretty plate for a more sophisticated setting. Though this easy appetizer certainly gets soft, I recommend serving it with crackers or pita chips that are sturdy enough to scoop, because the feta retains its firm texture.

I prefer to seek out feta that is from Greece or Israel (and, yes, it's easier than it sounds), as the flavor is a bit more complex. It seems to me that the big-name brands just taste like salt.

beets and greens with whipped feta spread

1 bunch beets (about 4 large), with greens attached

Olive oil, for coating the beets

1 tablespoon walnut or extra-virgin olive oil

2 teaspoons champagne vinegar

$^1/_2$ cup toasted pine nuts, plus more for garnish

Sea salt and freshly ground pepper

FETA SPREAD

$^1/_2$ cup (4 ounces) feta cheese, at room temperature

2 tablespoons cream cheese

2 tablespoons walnut or extra-virgin olive oil

1 tablespoon champagne vinegar

Whole milk, as needed

Preheat the oven to 425°F.

Cut off the beet greens flush with the top of each beet and set aside. Scrub the beets clean. Rub a bit of olive oil on the beets, wrap them all together tightly in foil, and bake until a toothpick stuck into the beets slides in and out with little resistance, 45 minutes to an hour. A good roasted beet is just tender, not cooked to death. Remove from the oven and set aside to cool.

To make the feta spread, in a food processor, pulse the feta a few times to break it up. Add the cream cheese, walnut oil, and vinegar and process until smooth. (Alternatively, use a strong arm and a whisk to break up the feta, then to beat all the ingredients together.) Add milk as needed to thin the mixture to a spreadable consistency.

Chop off the stalk of the beet greens, discarding any yellow pieces, and finely chop up the green parts. Toss the greens with the walnut oil, vinegar, the pine nuts, and a pinch of salt and pepper. Set in the fridge until ready to use.

When the beets are cool to the touch, peel off the skins, which should actually just slide off the flesh at this point. Slice the beets

A nice change from your usual crostini, this recipe uses roasted beet slices to stand in place of the toasted bread base. If you'd like to make this without cheese, you could top the roasted beets with the chopped greens alone, or just whip a nondairy cream cheese spread, although the feta adds a nice, salty richness to the snack. For even more punch, Gorgonzola works well too.

Both beets and beet greens have a distinctive taste that most people either love or hate. Some think their sweet earthiness is wonderful, but others find it a bit much. If I were having people over, I would include this among a variety of appetizers, as it is unapologetic in its beetiness. Keep in mind that beet juice is messy, and it stains, so when you plate these, commit to setting down each beet round in a certain place and assembling the dish from there, as things get muddled when you move them around too much. Messy as they are, beets save well, so you might want to roast some extras to have on hand as snacks. They should last up to 5 days in the fridge.

182   THE SPROUTED KITCHEN

horizontally into 1/4-inch rounds, discarding the end pieces so you are
left with even discs. Put the whipped cheese in a resealable plastic
bag and cut off a small corner to create a makeshift piping bag (it's
best to err on the small side, so you don't end up with a too-thick layer
of cheese on each beet). Pipe a ring of the whipped cheese around
the border of each beet and pile a heaping spoonful of the greens in
the center (the cheese border should help keep the greens in place).
Garnish with more pine nuts and serve at once.

mango guacamole with baked corn chips

SERVES 4 <

1 large shallot

1 ripe mango

Juice of 1 lime

1 serrano chile

2 avocados

Sea salt

1/2 cup cilantro, coarsely chopped

12 corn tortillas

1 tablespoon melted coconut oil or grapeseed oil

Finely chop the shallot, rinse, and drain in a fine-mesh strainer. Dab it dry with a paper towel.

Peel and pit the mango and dice into small pieces. In a large mixing bowl, combine the mango and lime juice. Stem and halve the serrano and remove some of the seeds (the seeds are what make the chile hot, so using all of them will be very spicy, half of them will be medium, and so on). Finely chop the serrano and add it to the mango mixture. Peel and pit the avocados and dice. Add the avocado, shallot, 1/2 teaspoon salt, and the cilantro to the bowl and mix. Taste and adjust the seasoning, if necessary. Keep chilled until ready to serve.

Arrange a rack in the upper third of your oven and preheat the oven to 375°F. Cut the tortillas into quarters. Combine them in a bowl with the oil and use your hands to toss to coat. Sprinkle generously with salt. Spread the tortillas on two baking sheets, arranging them so they overlap as little as possible. Bake both sheets in the upper third of the oven until lightly browned, rotating both sheets halfway through, 16 to 18 minutes.

Serve the bowl of mango guacamole with the chips alongside for dipping.

It seems like the bowl of guacamole, that ever-popular appetizer, is always the first thing to be emptied at a party. That's why you might want to double or triple the amounts for this chunky version made with sweet pieces of mango. In the unlikely event there is any remaining at the end of the night, the leftovers are fabulous on a goat cheese quesadilla.

Rinsing the shallot removes the sulfurous compounds that make it taste so strong. This step isn't crucial if you'll be enjoying it right away, but it's especially important if you're making the guacamole in advance. It a nice trick to tuck away the next time you're making anything with raw onions or garlic.

red grape salsa on crostini

1 Anaheim chile

About $^1/_2$ small red onion, finely diced

1$^1/_2$ pounds seedless red, blue, or black grapes, chilled

1 tablespoon red wine vinegar

1 heaping cup fresh cilantro, finely chopped

Sea salt and freshly ground pepper

1 whole grain baguette

4 ounces fresh goat cheese, at room temperature

2 tablespoons whole milk

Arrange a rack in the upper third of your oven and preheat the oven to 375°F.

Remove the stem and seeds from the Anaheim chile and dice as finely as possible. In a bowl, combine the chile and red onion (using a bit more or less, according to your taste). Dice the grapes. Add them to the bowl with the vinegar and $^1/_3$ cup of the cilantro and stir to combine. Add salt and pepper to taste and stir.

Slice the baguette on the diagonal into $^1/_4$-inch slices and arrange on a baking sheet. Bake until just toasted, about 4 minutes. Flip the crostini and continue baking until just toasted on that side, about 4 minutes more. Remove from the oven and let cool.

Put the goat cheese in a small bowl, add the milk, and stir until it reaches a spreadable consistency. Swipe one side of each baguette slice with about 1 scant tablespoon of the cheese and place a heaping spoonful of the grape salsa on top. Garnish with the remaining cilantro and serve immediately.

We shared this recipe

on the blog years ago and got such a positive response that I had to include it here. My sister has brought this great appetizer to a few family holiday parties, a gesture I find most flattering, and the unique combination has always gone over quite well.

The grape salsa can be made a few hours in advance but note that the flavor of the onion becomes a bit stronger as it sits. Be sure your grapes are very fresh and cold. This will make them easier to dice, as overripe or warm grapes will tend to collapse under the knife. If you can find red grapes in a variety of shades, the effect is just stunning. In the fall you can often find gorgeous black grapes and maybe some rich Concords. I just use a thin swipe of goat cheese on each baguette slice. If you like things a little heavier on the cheese, double the quantity.

roasted plum tartines

SERVES 8 <

6 ripe plums

Sea salt and freshly ground pepper

2 tablespoons honey, warmed

1$^1/_3$ cups ricotta cheese

$^1/_4$ cup freshly grated Parmesan
  cheese

3 tablespoons chopped fresh chives

1 whole grain baguette

1 cup microgreens, for garnish

Preheat the oven to 350°F and line a rimmed baking sheet with
parchment paper.

Cut the plums into quarters, removing the pits. Gently toss the plum
pieces with a pinch of salt and the warm honey. Spread them on the
prepared baking sheet, cut side up. Bake until the edges are crisped
and caramelized, 20 to 25 minutes. Remove from the oven and let cool.

While the plums are baking, in a bowl, stir together the ricotta,
Parmesan, chives, $^1/_4$ teaspoon salt, and a few grinds of pepper.

Turn the oven up to 500°F. Slice the baguette in half lengthwise. Place
the halves, cut side up, on a baking sheet and bake the bread just
until toasty, 4 to 5 minutes. Spread the ricotta mixture evenly on both
halves and return to the oven just until warmed through, another 1 to
2 minutes. Evenly distribute the roasted plums on top of the cheese.
Finish with a few grinds of pepper and garnish with the greens. Cut
each baguette half into slices on the diagonal. Serve warm or at room
temperature.

I do a few catering gigs
here and there, mostly for friends and
family. This is my most requested
appetizer in the summer, when stone
fruits are juicy and sweet. It may have
something to do with the fact that,
when I serve it to guests, I add finely
chopped cooked bacon to the ricotta
mixture, which tends to win a lot of
people over. I may not be a bacon
eater, but most people are really into
it. It's not included in the recipe here,
but if that sounds like your kind of
thing, throw some in. If you miss the
summer window for plums, try pears
or persimmons in the fall.

tofu summer rolls with cashew dipping sauce

SERVES 4 <

1 (14-ounce) package extra-firm tofu

1/4 cup toasted sesame seeds

6 leaves butter lettuce

Handful of Thai basil leaves

1 cucumber, cut into matchsticks

2 large carrots, grated

1/4 cup chopped fresh mint leaves

1 avocado, peeled, pitted, and thinly sliced

6 rice paper wrappers

DIPPING SAUCE

1/3 cup cashew butter

2 tablespoons agave nectar

1/4 cup low-sodium soy sauce or tamari

Juice of 1 lime

2 teaspoons Sriracha or chile-garlic sauce

Drain the tofu and wrap it in paper towels. Put it on a plate and weight it down with something heavy, like a heavy saucepan or a few large cans, to press out more of the moisture.

Meanwhile, to make the dipping sauce, whisk the cashew butter, agave nectar, soy sauce, lime juice, and Sriracha together in a bowl. Add water, 1 tablespoon at a time, until it is thin enough to use as a dipping sauce.

Cut the tofu into matchsticks about 4 inches long (the width of the tofu block) and 1 inch wide. Spread the sesame seeds on a plate and gently roll the tofu matchsticks in the seeds to coat. Set aside. Cut out the thick stem of each lettuce leaf and cut each leaf in half. Set out an assembly line of the basil, lettuce, cucumber, carrots, mint, avocado, and tofu in small bowls. Prepare a bowl of tepid water and a slightly damp dish towel to use as a work surface. Working with one wrapper at a time, soak the rice paper wrapper in the tepid water for about thirty seconds to soften. Lay it on the dish towel. Layer 2 basil leaves in the middle third of the circle. Keeping with the lengthwise

(continued)

If this is your first attempt at making summer rolls, be patient. Rice paper is a bit fussy to work with, and it will take you a few tries before you get a roll that looks decent. I've made a number of them now and mine still don't look authentic, but they taste great, and that's what matters. One of my testers mentioned that she has better luck with rice paper wrappers that have tapioca in them, as they don't tear quite as easily. While you're working, keep the finished rolls covered with a damp dish towel or paper towels to keep them from drying out.

I like the taste of tofu, but you could also use some grilled shrimp or chicken instead. Most health food stores and well-stocked grocery stores sell marinated tofu that has a firm texture; it works great as well to save a few minutes of prep time as you can just use the slices of tofu as they are, no draining or sesame seeds necessary. If you don't want to buy cashew butter for the sauce, creamy peanut butter is a fine alternative.

orientation, follow with a piece of lettuce, a couple of cucumber sticks, a few pinches of carrots, a pinch of the chopped mint, two slices of avocado, and a couple of the tofu matchsticks. Fold in both the top and bottom toward the center, roll the right flap over all the filling, and roll it up (like a burrito) until it sticks to the other side. Repeat with remaining wrappers and filling.

As each roll is done, place it under a damp paper towel until ready to serve. Slice them in half on the diagonal and serve with the cashew sauce on the side. They are best eaten immediately, but they can be stored, wrapped in plastic wrap, for up to a day.

two-bite grilled cheese

SERVES 4 TO 6 <

1 whole grain baguette

Extra-virgin olive oil, for brushing

1/2 cup apricot jam

10 slices Manchego cheese, each
about 1 inch by 3 inches

Sea salt

If you're using a grill pan instead of a griddle, preheat the oven to
200°F.

Slice the baguette on a slight diagonal, cutting slices that are thick
enough to hold together but thin enough that you will really be able
to taste the fillings. You should get about twenty 1/2-inch slices from
one baguette.

Brush one side of each baguette slice with olive oil. Spread the unoiled
sides of half of the slices with a scant 1/2 tablespoon of jam and top
with a slice of Manchego. Cover the Manchego with the remaining
baguette slices, oiled side up.

Heat your griddle or grill pan over medium heat. Working in batches
if necessary, grill the sandwiches until the cheese is melted and the
outsides are just toasted, about 11/2 minutes per side.

Transfer the sandwiches to the oven to keep them warm while
toasting the remaining sandwiches, if necessary. Sprinkle the tops
with salt and serve warm.

 A few other combinations you might want to try include:

· Fresh goat cheese, balsamic vinegar, and pear

· Gouda, apple, and whole grain mustard

· Sharp white cheddar, fresh basil, and roasted
tomatoes

· Gruyère, mozzarella, and a slice of roasted butternut
squash

A holiday party, a backyard
barbecue, or perhaps a night of appetizers and wine with close friends—
these are the sorts of occasions where
these miniature grilled cheese sandwiches belong. This combination is so
simple that it can hardly be called a
recipe, but I am telling you, these mini
versions of a fabulous flavor combination really hit the spot, and they
save you fuss in the kitchen when you
should be spending time with friends!

If you have a griddle, use it here to
make these most efficiently, but a grill
pan can be used as well. I like to prep
them all on a rimmed baking sheet so
they're all ready to grill up. You can use
the Quick Apricot Jam on page 24 if
you like, but store-bought jam works
just as well here.

cumin lentil dip in endive leaves

SERVES 4 TO 6 <

1 cup black or French green (du Puy) lentils, rinsed

2 cups water

2 shallots, chopped

2 teaspoons fennel seeds

1 heaping teaspoon ground cumin

1/2 cup Greek yogurt

1/4 cup chopped fresh fennel fronds or flat-leaf parsley, plus more for garnish

Smoked salt and freshly ground pepper

3 whole endives

Put the lentils in a saucepan with the water and bring to a gentle boil over medium-high heat. Reduce the heat to a simmer and cook, uncovered, until the lentils are tender, 15 to 20 minutes. Drain the lentils and set aside to cool to room temperature.

Using a nonstick pan over medium heat, dry-sauté the shallots, without oil, until slightly charred and softened a bit, about 6 minutes. Remove from the heat and place in a bowl. Break up the fennel seeds with the back of a knife and add to the bowl with the shallots. Add the lentils, cumin, and yogurt and stir to combine. Add the fennel fronds and a few generous pinches of salt and pepper. Taste and adjust flavors as you wish.

Gently pull the leaves from the endive at their stem. Fill the cavity of each endive leaf with a heaping spoonful of lentil dip and garnish with fresh fennel fronds.

There is a time and place to serve a warm, cheesy appetizer, but it's nice to have a few lighter options up your sleeve as well. Lighter, but still hearty with fiber-packed lentils, this dip is lovely served in endive leaves, as described here, but it is just as nice served on crackers or crostini.

You'll be glad you used freshly cooked lentils in this dish. Fairly delicate, lentils only take about 15 to 20 minutes to cook and retain their shape much better than canned ones, which are too wet and mushy to be used in this dip. A prepared package of steamed lentils will also work for this dish—just use 1 1/2 cups and skip the cooking step.

Treats

My sweet tooth is pretty persistent—it has a mind of its own, really. I wish I were enough of a health nut that I didn't give in as often as I do, but I eat dessert daily. The bit of control I do exercise is with the kinds of natural sweeteners and flours I use in baking and making other types of desserts. I try to replace white flour with whole grains and nut meals for more nutrition, and I use natural sweeteners such as turbinado sugar, maple syrup, and agave nectar where I can. Though some of these desserts are truly decadent, everything is on the lighter side compared to an average dessert. I was the one eating my way through all the recipes as I worked on this book, so I tried to keep an eye out for the both of us!

almond meal cookies with coconut and cacao nibs

MAKES 20 COOKIES <

1 1/4 cups almond meal

1/4 cup cacao nibs

1/2 cup unsweetened shredded coconut

1/2 teaspoon baking powder

1/4 teaspoon sea salt

1/3 cup muscovado sugar

1 egg

3 tablespoons coconut oil, melted

1/2 teaspoon pure vanilla extract

In a large mixing bowl, stir together the almond meal, cacao nibs, coconut, baking powder, salt, and sugar.

In another bowl, beat the egg very well until it is a uniform color and doubles in volume. Whisk in the coconut oil and vanilla extract. Add the wet mixture to the dry ingredients and mix until just combined. Put the bowl in the fridge and chill for at least 30 minutes, or up to overnight.

Preheat the oven to 375°F. Using your hands, roll the chilled dough into balls no larger than 1 inch in diameter and place on a baking sheet with 1 1/2-inch space between, giving them a gentle press on the tops to flatten just a bit. Bake until the edges just begin to brown, 7 to 10 minutes. Remove from the oven and let cool before serving.

In the world of gluten-free cookies, there are those that are amazing and those that miss the mark altogether. In this recipe, delicate almond meal results in a fabulous nutty cookie. Naturally tender, and almost chewy from the muscovado sugar, these cookies get a grown-up kick from the cacao nibs, which are not as sweet as chocolate chips and have a toasty, almost espresso-like flavor.

These cookies are just a hair away from being vegan as well. If you'd like them to be, you could replace the egg with Ener-G Egg Replacer or a mixture of 1 tablespoon of ground flaxseed (flax meal) and 3 tablespoons of water. The alternatives don't have quite as much leavening power as the eggs, but they will help act as a binder.

Don't use a nonstick silicone baking mat or parchment paper here, as the bit of crust on the bottom of each cookie helps keep the delicate treats together. Smaller cookies will also hold together better than larger ones.

dairy-free lemon crèmes with oat-thyme crumble

MAKES 4 <

1 (12.3-ounce) package extra-firm silken tofu

2 tablespoons fine or medium-ground cornmeal

Pinch of sea salt

1/3 to 1/2 cup honey

Grated zest of 1 Meyer lemon

3 tablespoons freshly squeezed Meyer lemon juice

OAT CRUMBLE

2 tablespoons coconut oil

1/4 teaspoon pure vanilla extract

1/4 cup natural cane sugar

1/4 teaspoon sea salt

1/2 cup old-fashioned rolled oats

1/4 cup chopped raw almonds

1 tablespoon fresh thyme leaves

Wrap the tofu between a few layers of paper towels and set aside to drain for 10 minutes. In a food processor or in a bowl using a whisk, blend the tofu, cornmeal, salt, honey, and lemon zest and juice until completely smooth, about 1 minute if using a food processor. Divide the mixture among four small bowls and refrigerate for at least 2 hours. This can be done up to a day in advance.

Preheat the oven to 350°F.

To make the oat crumble, melt the coconut oil until liquid in a small saucepan or in the microwave. In a bowl, stir together the coconut oil, vanilla, sugar, and salt. Add the oats and almonds and stir to coat everything evenly. Rub half of the thyme leaves between your fingers to release their fragrance and stir them in. Spread the mixture on a rimmed baking sheet and bake until dry and just toasted, about 20 minutes. Set aside to cool.

Once the crèmes are chilled, sprinkle the cooled crumble on top, garnish with the remaining thyme, and serve.

I took this dessert over to my parents' house for them to taste before I told them the main ingredient. My Dad loves to tease that all of my "hippie healthy" dishes are inferior to his classic American fare, but I watched him scrape the bowl clean before I victoriously told him it was made with tofu. I'm not saying he would choose this over a hot fudge sundae, but he ate it without reservation.

I have found that different types of honey yield different levels of sweetness. Start with 1/3 cup, taste the mixture, and adjust from there. If you want to keep this strictly vegan, the honey could be replaced with agave nectar. Be sure to use only silken tofu in this dish. It is sold in shelf-stable packages, likely near the Asian foods in your grocery store. The tofu that is sold in the refrigerator case, though made of the same ingredients, is processed differently and has a more distinct soybean flavor and grittier texture. Lastly, though only a small amount is used here, keep in mind that stone-ground cornmeal contains more flavor and nutrition than the steel-ground variety.

almond meal–strawberry cake

SERVES 8 <

3 eggs

1 vanilla bean

1/4 cup honey

3/4 cup Greek yogurt

3 tablespoons unsalted butter, melted and cooled slightly

2 cups almond meal

1/2 cup whole wheat pastry flour or gluten-free all-purpose flour

1/3 cup natural cane sugar

1/2 teaspoon freshly grated nutmeg

1 teaspoon baking soda

1/2 teaspoon baking powder

3/4 teaspoon sea salt

WHIPPED TOPPING

1 cup heavy cream

1 tablespoon natural cane sugar, or more as needed

1/2 tablespoon pure vanilla extract

1/2 cup mascarpone cheese

Sea salt

2 cups sliced strawberries, slightly mashed

Toasted sliced almonds, for garnish

Preheat the oven to 325°F. Grease a 9-inch round cake pan and line the bottom with parchment paper.

In a bowl, whisk the eggs well. Halve the vanilla bean lengthwise and scrape the seeds into the eggs. Discard the bean or save for another use. Add the honey, yogurt, and butter and whisk again. In another bowl, sift together the almond meal, flour, sugar, nutmeg, baking soda, baking powder, and salt. Mix the wet ingredients into the dry and pour the batter into the prepared cake pan. Bake until a toothpick inserted into the center of the cake comes out clean, 22 to 25 minutes. Set aside to cool completely, then invert onto a cooling rack.

While the cake is baking, whip the cream with a handheld electric mixer until it begins to thicken, then add the sugar and vanilla and continue to beat until fluffy. In the final minute, beat in the mascarpone and a pinch of salt. Taste and whip in more sugar, if you like.

Top the cake with the cream mixture, leaving a 1-inch border uncovered. Top with the strawberries and almonds, and serve.

For me, one of the best things about cooking is the magic that can happen when you combine the right flavors, like peanut butter and chocolate or strawberries and cream. This cake has three parts: the cake, the mascarpone cream, and the strawberries. On their own, they are good, but together they are simply delightful.

When people are coming over for dinner, I prefer to serve a dessert that is already assembled so I don't have to get up and work while the conversation is at its best. The cake can be made in advance, with the cream whipped up and the berries added just before serving. This could be made lighter by topping it with honey-sweetened Greek yogurt instead of the mascarpone mixture. Cake for breakfast, anyone?

chocolate-drizzled
oatmeal shortbread

MAKES 20 COOKIES <

1¹/₂ cups old-fashioned rolled oats, plus more for garnish (optional)

¹/₂ cup unsalted butter, at room temperature

¹/₂ cup turbinado sugar, plus more for garnish (optional)

2 teaspoons pure vanilla extract

1 egg

³/₄ cup unbleached all-purpose or rice flour

¹/₄ teaspoon sea salt

¹/₂ teaspoon freshly grated nutmeg

2¹/₂ ounces dark chocolate (60% to 72% cacao), chopped

Flaked sea salt, such as Maldon, for garnish (optional)

In a food processor, pulse the oats to create a coarse flour. You want a bit of texture to remain, not pureed until it is completely smooth. Set aside.

In the food processor or using a bowl and wooden spoon, cream the butter and sugar together. Add the vanilla and egg and mix again. Add the oat flour, all-purpose flour, salt, and nutmeg and pulse a few times to combine, scraping down the sides of the food processor or your bowl as necessary. The dough will be fairly tacky.

Using your hands, roll the dough into a uniform log about 3 inches in diameter. If you like, sprinkle a handful of rolled oats and a few tablespoons of turbinado sugar on your work surface and roll the log in the mixture to create a crust. Roll the log up in plastic wrap or parchment paper and chill in the fridge for at least 1 hour, and preferably 2.

Preheat the oven to 350°F and line a baking sheet with parchment paper.

Working quickly, slice the log into ¹/₂-inch coins and spread them on the baking sheet 2 inches apart. Bake until the edges just begin to brown, 14 to 16 minutes. Transfer the cookies to a wire rack.

I was a Girl Scout for years, and I definitely stood in front of markets and went door to door selling those popular cookies, which, now that I know better, I feel bad about pushing on people. I was a Thin Mints girl, and we kept them in the freezer to give them an even better crunch. I was also intrigued by the shortbread Trefoils, which had a one-dimensional flavor, really, but had a sandy texture and almost melted in your mouth.

Now that I prefer the taste of homemade cookies to packaged ones, I like to make this variation on traditional shortbread, with oats that give it a coarser texture and a good snap. I make a coarse oat flour by grinding old-fashioned oats in a food processor. Otherwise, you can purchase oat flour and stir in some whole oats for texture. And while we're straying from tradition, a bit of chocolate is always welcome in my cookies, so I drizzle a bit on here. If there were ever a time to use organic butter and good-quality chocolate, now would be it.

As for putting these in the freezer, a batch hasn't gone uneaten long enough to try.

Melt the chocolate in a heatproof glass bowl over a pot of simmering water, being careful not to let the bottom of the bowl touch the water. Arrange the piece of parchment you used for cooking the cookies under the wire rack for easy cleanup. Drizzle the melted chocolate on the tops of the cookies in a zig-zag motion. I find this easiest to do by putting the slightly cooled chocolate in a resealable plastic bag, snipping off a tiny nip at the corner to create a makeshift pastry bag, and drizzling it from there. You can use a small spoon as well, with a bit more of a rustic result. Sprinkle a bit of flaked salt on the top of each cookie. The chocolate will firm up in about 15 to 20 minutes. Store the cookies in an airtight container for up to 1 week.

peanut butter pretzel tartlets

MAKES 20 TO 24 TARTLETS <

About 2 cups whole grain pretzel sticks

$1/4$ cup cold unsalted butter, cut into small cubes, plus more for the tins

$1/2$ teaspoon pure vanilla extract

$1/3$ cup muscovado sugar

1 egg yolk

2 ounces dark chocolate (60% to 72% cacao)

$1/4$ cup heavy cream

$1/3$ cup creamy natural peanut butter

$1/4$ cup confectioners' sugar, if needed

$1/4$ cup toasted, salted peanuts

Flaked sea salt, such as Maldon, for garnish

In a food processor, pulse the pretzel pieces until they form a coarse meal. Don't worry if there are a few small chunks remaining. Measure the pulverized pretzels; you should have $1^1/2$ cups. Adjust the quantity, if necessary. Add the cold butter, vanilla, sugar, and egg yolk to the food processor and pulse until just combined. Add water, 1 tablespoon at a time, until the mixture sticks together. Alternatively, you could pulverize the pretzels in a blender and combine them with the butter, vanilla, sugar, and egg yolk, using a pastry cutter, then stir in the water 1 tablespoon at a time. Chill the mixture in the fridge for 20 minutes.

Preheat the oven to 350°F. Grease two mini-muffin tins with butter.

Press a heaping tablespoonful of the crust mixture into each well of the muffin tins, making sure to press it into the corners, so that there is a thin layer of crust on the bottom and up the sides. Even out the edge on the top by pressing it down a bit with your fingers. Bake the crusts until dry and barely golden, 12 to 14 minutes. Remove from the oven and let cool completely.

While the crusts are cooling, break the chocolate into small pieces in a heatproof glass bowl. In a small saucepan, warm the cream just barely to a simmer and pour the hot cream over the chocolate. Let it sit for a minute, and then gently stir until the chocolate is uniformly melted.

Both peanut butter–filled and chocolate-covered pretzels are favorites in our house, and this is sort of the marriage of the two. Salty pretzels go into the crust, which is dressed up with a peanut butter cup filling—perfect for when you just want a few bites of something sweet, or you're having a get-together where people are grazing more than sitting down to dessert.

Don't use miniature pretzels for the crust. They are too firm and don't pulverize like the larger ones. I like using the honey wheat sticks from Trader Joe's. Also, I find that the consistency of natural peanut butter varies greatly. If it is on the firmer side, I'll use the peanut butter as is. If it's runnier, mix in $1/4$ cup confectioners' sugar to make the peanut butter layer firmer.

Remove the tart shells from the muffin tins and place them on a serving tray. If the peanut butter is somewhat runny, stir in the confectioners' sugar to firm it up. Using a small spoon, dollop 1/2 teaspoon of the peanut butter into each tart shell. Use a clean spoon to cover the peanut butter layer with a spoonful of the chocolate ganache. You should have enough to fill each tart to the top.

Put a peanut on top of each tart and sprinkle with the salt. Chill in the fridge for 20 minutes to set. They can be kept covered in the fridge for 2 to 3 days.

cocoa hazelnut cupcakes

MAKES 12 CUPCAKES

1 cup hazelnut meal

3/4 cup muscovado sugar

1/2 cup natural (nonalkalized) cocoa powder

1/3 cup whole wheat pastry flour

1/2 teaspoon baking powder

1/2 teaspoon baking soda

1/2 teaspoon sea salt

2 eggs

3 tablespoons unsalted butter, melted and slightly cooled

1/4 cup unsweetened applesauce

2 teaspoons pure vanilla extract

3/4 cup low-fat buttermilk

1/2 cup semisweet chocolate chips

WHIPPED FROSTING

1 cup cold heavy cream

1/3 cup muscovado sugar, or more as needed

1 teaspoon pure vanilla extract

2/3 cup hazelnut butter

Pinch of sea salt

Chopped toasted hazelnuts, for garnish

Shaved dark chocolate (60% to 72% cacao), for garnish

Preheat the oven to 350°F. Line a muffin tin with paper liners.

Sift together the hazelnut meal, muscovado sugar, cocoa powder, pastry flour, baking powder, baking soda, and salt in a large mixing bowl. In a separate bowl, whisk together the eggs and stir in the melted butter, applesauce, vanilla, and buttermilk until combined. Stir the wet mixture into the dry ingredients until combined, being careful not to overmix. Stir in the chocolate chips. Divide the mixture between the wells of the muffin tin, filling each about halfway full. Bake, rotating the pan halfway through, until an inserted toothpick comes out clean, 20 to 22 minutes (they will be moister than a standard cake at first, as they dry a tad more as they sit). Remove from the oven and set on a wire rack to cool.

While the cupcakes cool, prepare the frosting. In a stand mixer or using a handheld electric mixer, whip the cream until peaks begin

(continued)

Popular chocolate-and-hazelnut spread Nutella is not the most wholesome thing on the shelf, but the combination of chocolate and hazelnuts, in general, is really something.

I use muscovado sugar in the frosting, which lends a hint of caramel flavor but tends to result in a grittier texture than confectioners' sugar would. If you prefer a smoother texture, substitute about 1 cup of confectioners' sugar for the muscovado.

The cupcakes are best eaten the day they are made. Nut meals tend to absorb moisture as they sit, making baked goods dry out fairly quickly. The frosting has whipping cream in it, so prepare it no more than a few hours before serving.

to form, then add the sugar and vanilla while you continue to whip. Once you see stiff peaks, gently add the hazelnut butter and salt and whip just to combine. Note that if you made your own hazelnut butter, it must be completely cooled before adding. Also, the addition of the heavy nut butter will deflate the cream, so be as gentle as possible. Taste and adjust the sweetness, if desired. The cupcakes and frosting can be prepared to this point up to a few hours in advance, with the frosting kept in the fridge until ready to serve.

Once the cupcakes are completely cooled, top them with the frosting and garnish with chopped hazelnuts and shaved chocolate. The cupcakes are best served the day they are made.

Hazelnut meal can be tough to find, and it's a tad pricey when you do, so I make small batches in the food processor. You just put skinned nuts into a food processor and run it until they are broken down to an almost flourlike consistency. If it goes too long, however, you'll end up with hazelnut butter (which isn't such a bad thing, as you do need some of that for the frosting), so be sure to stop short and pull out the hazelnut meal before the oils break down. If you are making your own hazelnut butter for the frosting instead of purchasing it, add a touch of neutral-tasting oil and keep running the processor to help smooth the nut butter out.

grilled peaches with maple crème fraîche

SERVES 6 <

3 ripe peaches

1 teaspoon coconut oil or unsalted butter, at room temperature

3/4 cup crème fraîche

2 tablespoons maple syrup, or more as needed

1/2 cup crushed gingersnap cookies

Heat your grill or grill pan over medium-high heat. Halve each peach and, using your finger, rub the coconut oil onto the exposed flesh of each half.

In a bowl, whisk together the crème fraîche and maple syrup. If your peaches are sweet, this should be sweet enough, but you can add a bit more maple syrup if you wish. Set in the fridge until ready to use.

Grill each of the peach halves, cut side down, for 2 minutes. Turn each half 90 degrees, to make crisscrossed grill marks, and grill another 1 to 2 minutes. Transfer each half to a shallow bowl or plate, spoon a generous dollop of the maple crème fraîche on top, and sprinkle with the crushed gingersnaps. Serve immediately.

You can probably tell

by this point that I am a fan of fruit in both sweet and savory recipes. I can eat berries by the pint, and I go through enough cherries to create a mountain of pits, but there is absolutely nothing in the world like a perfectly ripe late-summer peach. Nothing.

This simple dessert has the potential to be incredible—*if* you can find fabulous peaches. I like making this dessert for outdoor dinner parties, as it doesn't require much work at all. You can make the maple cream in advance, so all you have to do before serving is throw the peaches on the grill for a few minutes. If you're avoiding gluten, you can use gluten-free gingersnaps or even toasted pecans. If you want something a bit lighter, substitute Greek yogurt—preferably full- or low-fat—for the crème fraîche.

coconut lime tart

SERVES 6 TO 8 <

CRUST

1 cup old-fashioned rolled oats

$1/4$ cup spelt flour

$1/3$ cup unsalted toasted pistachios

1 tablespoon honey

5 tablespoons coconut oil

$1/2$ teaspoon sea salt

1 to 2 tablespoons water

FILLING

1 (13.5-ounce) can coconut milk

$1/3$ cup natural cane sugar

Grated zest and juice of 1 lime

1 tablespoon coconut flour or
   3 tablespoons brown rice flour or
   unbleached all-purpose flour

1 egg

1 egg yolk

$1/4$ teaspoon sea salt

$1/2$ teaspoon pure vanilla extract

Toasted shredded coconut, for garnish

Line the bottom of a 14 by 5-inch tart pan with a removable bottom with parchment paper. Combine the oats, spelt flour, and pistachios in a food processor and pulse to create a coarse flour. Add the honey, coconut oil, and salt and pulse a few times to combine. Add the water, 1 tablespoon at a time, and pulse until the mixture just begins to hold together. Immediately press the crust into the bottom and just barely up the sides of the prepared tart pan in a thin, even layer. Put in the fridge to chill for at least 1 hour, and up to 5 hours.

Preheat the oven to 375°F.

Pierce the bottom of the crust with a fork a few times and bake just until toasty, 12 to 14 minutes. Set aside and let cool completely.

Turn the oven down to 325°F. To make the filling, put the coconut milk in a small saucepan and bring to a simmer. Simmer for 5 minutes. Turn off the heat, then stir in the sugar and lime zest and sift in the flour. After the mixture has cooled slightly, whisk in the lime juice, egg, egg yolk, salt, and vanilla until completely combined. Let cool to room temperature. Strain the mixture through a fine-mesh strainer

My favorite desserts usually include chocolate and/or ice cream, but it's nice to have options for the few who prefer other sorts of sweets. This tart has a crisp, nutty crust and a custardlike filling and is finished with a generous sprinkle of toasted coconut.

Don't use light coconut milk in this recipe, since it has a thinner consistency and doesn't set up with as much success. However, a few different types of flour may be used in the filling, as it is simply there to help set the ingredients, not for flavor. I make this in a rectangular tart pan with a removable bottom, but I imagine you could make it in an 8-inch square as well. The baking time may vary, however, so keep an eye on it.

and pour into the crust. Bake until the center of the filling is just set, 23 to 25 minutes. Remove from the oven and let cool to room temperature, garnish with the toasted coconut, then chill in the fridge for at least 20 minutes before serving.

goat cheese panna cotta with roasted figs

SERVES 6 <

2 teaspoons powdered gelatin

3 tablespoons tepid water

1 cup whole milk

$^1/_2$ cup honey

4 ounces fresh goat cheese, at room temperature

$1^1/_4$ cups Greek yogurt

$^1/_2$ teaspoon pure vanilla extract

9 to 12 fresh figs

1 tablespoon turbinado sugar

$^1/_3$ cup toasted pistachios, coarsely chopped

In a small glass bowl, sprinkle the gelatin over the water and let it sit.

Meanwhile, in a small saucepan over medium-low heat, warm the milk and honey until bubbles start to form at the edges and the honey has dissolved. Remove from the heat. Crumble in the goat cheese and stir in the dissolved gelatin. After it cools just slightly, stir in the yogurt and vanilla. Pour through a fine-mesh strainer into a bowl. Coat six 6- to 8-ounce ramekins with a neutral-tasting oil, such as coconut oil. Divide the mixture among the ramekins. Cover and chill in the fridge for at least 3 hours and up to overnight.

Preheat the oven to 400°F and line a rimmed baking sheet with parchment paper. Halve the figs lengthwise and arrange on the prepared baking sheet cut side up. Sprinkle them with the sugar and roast until they are just starting to break down but still hold their shape, 8 to 10 minutes. Remove from the oven and let cool.

To serve, dip the bottom of each ramekin in hot water, run a butter knife around the edge, and invert the panna cotta onto a plate. Alternatively, serve the panna cottas in the ramekins. Top each serving with the figs and pistachios.

I remember making panna cotta for the first time. A few of my girlfriends and I were traveling in Italy, where we took a private cooking class from this spunky Italian woman we had heard about at the market. The class was in an attic that had been turned into a kitchen, and I can vividly remember our instructor hanging out the window, smoking out into the rain from the top floor, as we waited for the panna cotta to set. I stared at my plate thinking this was just an Italian word for a Jell-O mold, but upon tasting it I realized it had a delicate creaminess with the potential to beautifully complete a special meal. If you want show-stopping decadence, this is not it. However, if you want a delicately creamy dish that's just sweet enough to finish off a great meal, then this is the dessert for you. Even here in California, the land of the long growing season, we have a short window for fresh figs. You can make this recipe with sweet black cherries in the late spring and summer or bosc pears in the fall months. Those who don't eat gelatin can use agar, a vegetarian alternative made from seaweed that can be found at natural foods stores. To use, dissolve about 1 teaspoon of agar powder into the warm milk.

inside-out apple pie à la mode

SERVES 6 <

OAT CRUST

1 cup old-fashioned rolled oats

1/2 cup chopped raw pecans

1/2 cup muscovado sugar

1/2 teaspoon sea salt

1 teaspoon ground cinnamon

1/4 cup unsalted butter, melted

FILLING

1 quart premium vanilla bean ice cream

TOPPING

3 tablespoons unsalted butter

4 large tart apples, peeled, cored, and sliced

1/4 cup muscovado sugar

1/4 teaspoon ground cinnamon

1 teaspoon pure vanilla extract

Chopped toasted pecans or granola, for garnish (optional)

Preheat the oven to 375°F.

To make the crust, stir together the oats, pecans, muscovado sugar, salt, and cinnamon in a large bowl. Add the melted butter and stir to combine. Press the mixture into the bottom and up the sides of a 9-inch pie pan and bake until toasted, 10 to 12 minutes. Remove from the oven and use the back of a spoon to push the crust back up the sides, as it will have fallen a bit, and set on a wire rack to cool completely.

Remove the ice cream from the freezer and allow it to soften for about 10 minutes. Scoop the ice cream into the pie shell and spread it in an even layer. I find this works best by using a large spoon and dipping it in warm water every so often to help spread the ice cream out flat. Put the pie back in the freezer to firm up for at least 1 hour, or up to 3 days, placing a piece of plastic wrap on top if you'll be freezing it for more than a few hours.

To make the topping, melt the butter in a large sauté pan. Add the apple slices and sauté until tender, 8 to 10 minutes. Add the

The contrasts in both temperature and texture—from the crunchy crust, to the cold ice cream, to the warm apples—put this ice cream pie in a class all its own. And, believe it or not, all the components can be made in advance, so all you have to do is simply warm up the apples when you're ready to serve. If you or someone you're serving has a nut allergy, 1/2 cup more oats can be substituted for the pecans in the crust.

Note that if you put all the warm apples on top of the ice cream pie, you will end up with a big mess. I suggest cutting the pie into pieces and serving each with an individual scoop of warm apples. Alternatively, you can serve the sautéed apples at room temperature, which will keep the ice cream from melting so quickly.

muscovado sugar, cinnamon, and vanilla and continue cooking until a sauce forms, another 2 minutes.

Remove the ice cream pie from the freezer, cut into six pieces, wiping off your knife between each slice, and spoon the warm apples on top of each slice. Alternatively, let the apples cool to room temperature and then pile them onto the ice cream pie before cutting into serving pieces. Garnish with the pecans or granola and serve immediately.

flourless chocolate-banana pudding cakes with cinnamon cream

SERVES 6 <

3 ounces good-quality dark chocolate (60% to 72% cacao), chopped

2.5 ounces good-quality milk chocolate, chopped

2 very ripe bananas

1 egg, beaten

1/2 teaspoon pure vanilla extract

1/4 cup natural cane sugar

1/2 teaspoon sea salt

2 egg whites

WHIPPED CREAM

1 cup cold heavy cream

2 tablespoons natural cane sugar

1/4 teaspoon ground cinnamon

Preheat the oven to 350°F. Grease six (6-ounce) ramekins with butter and set aside.

Combine both chocolates in a heatproof glass bowl over a pot of simmering water, being careful not to let the bottom of the bowl touch the water. Stir the chocolate with a silicone spatula until it is uniformly melted, 8 to 10 minutes. Set the bowl aside to cool slightly.

In a large mixing bowl, mash the bananas very well; you want them as smooth as possible. Add the egg, vanilla, cane sugar, and salt and stir to combine. Gently stir in the melted chocolate until combined.

In another bowl, whip the egg whites with a stand mixer or handheld electric mixer until stiff peaks form. Gently fold the egg whites into the chocolate mixture in a few big sweeps to avoid deflating the batter. It is okay if some streaks remain. Divide the mixture among the ramekins and place the ramekins in a 9 by 13-inch pan. Fill the pan with boiling water that reaches about halfway up the sides of the ramekins. Bake until the tops of the cakes are set, 20 to 22 minutes.

Although I am all for some decadence here and there, I eat treats quite frequently, which is why I like desserts like this little pudding cake, which is only lightly sweetened but still chocolatey enough to hit the spot. The texture hovers somewhere around that of a mousse or a sponge cake, being both moist and airy but still rich in chocolate flavor. I bake the banana-flecked cakes in a water bath to keep them moist and delicate—almost custardlike. When I say "very ripe banana" here, I mean one that is brown, super-sweet, and very fragrant. If you want a dairy-free dessert, I would recommend substituting rice or soy ice cream for the whipped cream, since the chocolate in this dish really benefits by being served with something creamy.

To make the whipped cream, whip the cream using a stand mixer or a handheld electric mixture until it holds its shape. Sprinkle in the cane sugar and cinnamon and continue to whip for 1 minute more. Serve each cake in its ramekin topped with a dollop of whipped cream.

oatmeal ice cream sandwiches

MAKES 15 SANDWICHES ‹

¹/₂ cup unsalted butter, at room temperature

¹/₄ cup dark muscovado sugar

¹/₄ cup natural cane sugar

1 egg

2 tablespoons honey

1 cup creamy natural peanut butter

1¹/₃ cups oat flour

¹/₂ teaspoon baking soda

¹/₂ teaspoon sea salt

1 cup semisweet chocolate chips, coarsely chopped

2 quarts premium vanilla bean ice cream

1 cup chopped roasted peanuts, for garnish (optional)

With an electric mixer, cream the butter and sugars together until fluffy. Add the egg, honey, and peanut butter and mix until well combined. In a large mixing bowl, combine the oat flour, baking soda, salt, and chocolate chips. Add the wet ingredients to the dry and stir until just combined. Chill in the fridge for at least 1 hour.

Preheat the oven to 350°F. Line two baking sheets with parchment paper.

Roll the dough into 1¹/₂-inch balls and place them on a baking sheet 2 inches apart, using a second baking sheet as necessary. You should have about 30 cookies. Bake, rotating the trays halfway through, until the outer edges turn golden, 8 to 10 minutes. Transfer to a wire rack and let cool. Once cooled, transfer to plates and chill in the freezer for at least 20 minutes.

Remove the ice cream from the freezer and let soften for a few minutes. Using an ice cream scoop, place one scoop of ice cream on the bottom of a cookie and top it with another cookie. Gently press down and smooth the outer edge. Roll the ice cream edge in the peanuts, pressing them to adhere, and place the sandwich back on one of the plates in the freezer. Repeat. Once fully frozen, after 20 to 30 minutes, wrap tightly in plastic wrap or parchment paper. They will keep in the freezer for up to a month.

Making this recipe

requires a little bit of time, since you'll have to wait for some of the ingredients to chill, but once they are made, they'll keep in the freezer for up to a month, so you'll have an ice cream sandwich whenever you please. It's such a special treat to have these waiting in the freezer when someone pops over. The cookies are pretty tender, so I freeze them before I put the ice cream between. They never get rock hard in the freezer, so even on the first bite you can enjoy them without hurting your teeth.

I find that a thinner, more fluid natural peanut butter, such as Laura Scudder's Organic Smooth Peanut Butter, works best. You can purchase oat flour, but I love the convenience of making it myself, and the texture of homemade oat flour is quite lovely. To yield the amount you need for this recipe, pulse about 1¹/₄ cups old-fashioned rolled oats in a food processor until it looks like a coarse flour.

fresh mint chip frozen yogurt

SERVES 4 <

1 cup fresh mint leaves

1 cup heavy cream

1/2 cup plus 2 tablespoons brown rice syrup

Scant 1/2 teaspoon peppermint extract

2 cups whole-milk Greek yogurt

2 ounces good-quality dark chocolate, finely chopped

Coarsely chop the mint leaves and put them in a saucepan with the cream. Bring just to a simmer over medium heat, occasionally stirring and pressing the mint leaves so that they release the oils. As soon as it comes to a simmer, add the brown rice syrup and stir to combine, then turn off the heat. Leave the mixture on the stove top to steep for 30 minutes.

Pour the cream mixture into a bowl through a fine-mesh sieve to remove the mint leaves. Add the peppermint extract and yogurt to the bowl and whisk to combine. Cover the mixture and chill in the fridge for at least 30 minutes and up to overnight.

Churn the yogurt mixture in an ice cream maker, following the manufacturer's instructions. When the yogurt is finished churning, stir in the chocolate. Transfer the frozen yogurt to a covered container and store in the freezer, where it will firm up. It tastes best after just 1 hour in the freezer. If it hardens completely, remove it from the freezer 15 minutes before serving to make it easier to scoop.

A typical ice cream base

has egg yolks or corn syrup to help with the viscosity, but this healthier version works with the thickness of Greek yogurt plus brown rice syrup as the sweetener. Unlike most frozen yogurt recipes, this one has cream in it, but it's for a good reason. I wanted to include fresh mint in this recipe, and to get that flavor into the yogurt I had to infuse the mint into a liquid. Coconut milk will work, too, but the bit of cream makes this dessert lusciously smooth. It certainly tastes of yogurt, but the cream—and the shards of chocolate throughout—lead it into the treat category and away from your breakfast routine. After many test batches, I settled on using a combination of fresh mint and mint extract. The fresh mint imparts an herbal element, while the mint extract gives you the bold flavor that you expect in mint ice cream. You could certainly double it and go with just one. The lower the fat content of your yogurt, the icier the result will be. If you plan to eat this dessert straight from the machine, low-fat yogurt will work, but if it's going to be in the freezer for some time, using whole yogurt prevents it from turning into one giant ice cube. In either case, it's best enjoyed sooner rather than later.

acai sorbet

SERVES 4 <

2 ripe bananas

Sea salt

2 tablespoons agave nectar

2 (100-gram) packets frozen acai
    puree, thawed

Juice of $1/2$ orange

2 tablespoons champagne or vodka
    (optional)

In a bowl, mash the bananas and a small pinch of salt very well with a fork or potato masher until smooth. Add the agave nectar, acai puree, orange juice, and champagne to the bowl and stir to combine. Churn the mixture in an ice cream maker, following the manufacturer's instructions. Serve immediately, or transfer to a covered container and store in the freezer for up to a week.

A health trend a year or two ago recommended churning ripe bananas into an ice cream maker, which yields a very light alternative to ice cream. As an ice cream fan, I can't say it really compares, but this vegan treat is ridiculously simple to make and provides an infallible excuse for eating ice cream for breakfast. In this version, the tartness of the acai and orange juice provide a welcome contrast to the creamy banana.

The champagne used here is not for the flavor but for the texture. It's totally optional, but it helps the sorbet remain scoopable. This dish is best eaten freshly churned, but it can be kept in the freezer for a few days. Just take it out a few minutes before serving so it softens. Acai puree comes in individual frozen packets and can be found at health food stores and larger supermarkets.

Etc.

I wanted to wrap up this book with a few staples that are convenient to have on hand. Basic cooking techniques are important to master in order to achieve a solid foundation upon which to build. I experiment with ease in my cooking because I have messed up enough times to make some sort of improvement the next time. Everyone, whether a beginner in the kitchen, an accomplished home cook, or a professional chef, has something to learn about cooking. The only way to become confident in the kitchen is to cook often, try different things, learn from the mistakes, and build your repertoire from the ground up.

roasted garlic

MAKES ABOUT 10 CLOVES <

1 head garlic
2 teaspoons extra-virgin olive oil

Pinch of sea salt
1 sprig rosemary (optional)

Preheat the oven to 400°F.

Cut off about ¼ inch from the top of the head of garlic, just enough to expose the tops of the cloves. Drizzle the oil on top of the garlic and rub it in thoroughly. Sprinkle the salt on top.

Place the rosemary sprig, if using, on top of the head of garlic and wrap loosely in a piece of foil or parchment paper. Bake until the cloves are softened, 40 to 45 minutes.

Use immediately, squeezing the garlic cloves out of their skin, or store in a covered container with just enough olive oil to cover, for up to 2 weeks. (Remember that the oil is useful, too!)

Although roasting garlic takes only a few minutes of actual hands-on time, it results in a rich, caramelized spreadable garlic that doesn't have the kick of raw cloves. If you throw a wrapped head in the oven whenever the oven is already on anyway, you'll be glad to have it around. It spreads easily and it doesn't have quite the lasting effect on your breath as raw garlic. I use it on garlic bread, in salad dressing, on pizza, and in any dish with potatoes.

caramelized onions

2 large yellow onions
1 tablespoon extra-virgin olive oil
Sea salt

Peel the onions and slice into thin rings, discarding the tough ends.

Heat the oil in a large sauté pan over medium heat. You'll want to use the largest pan you have, as the more spread out the onions are the more they will brown. When the oil begins to shimmer, add the onions to the pan. They will crowd the pan at first, but soon they'll cook down significantly. Once the onions have softened and cooked down a bit, add a few pinches of salt, turn the heat to medium-low, and continue to cook, stirring every few minutes until brown and the onions smell fragrant and sweet, about 30 minutes.

Use them immediately, or let cool completely, transfer to a covered container, and store in the fridge for up to 10 days.

When a vegetarian dish

is lacking in depth, I find that I often reach for certain condiments to do the trick, such as sautéed mushrooms, smoked paprika, miso, roasted garlic, and Parmesan cheese. Caramelized onions have got to be near the top of the list, as they give a savory, almost smoky flavor to vegetables and beans. The pan doesn't need a lot of oil since the onions release their own liquid as they cook—it takes a good thirty minutes to bring out the onions' natural sugars and cook them down.

Keep these in the fridge and use them to dress up a number of dishes. I put them on sandwiches, and they go great with potato and cauliflower dishes or as a topping on pizzas. If you like, you can add a splash of balsamic vinegar in the last few minutes of cooking.

herb compound butter

$^1/_2$ cup unsalted butter

1 tablespoon fresh chives

2 tablespoons fresh flat-leaf parsley

2 tablespoons fresh tarragon

1 tablespoon grated lemon zest

Sea salt and freshly ground pepper

Remove the butter from the fridge and allow it to come to room temperature or a few degrees below. Put the chives, parsley, and tarragon in a pile on your cutting board and finely chop them all together. Gather the herbs together in a pile again, add the butter and lemon zest on top, and, using a sharp knife, chop and scrape the mixture until everything is combined. Add a pinch of salt and pepper and chop and scrape to combine one more time.

Roll the mixture into a log and place it on the front edge of a piece of parchment paper or plastic wrap. Fold the edge over and roll, twisting the ends of parchment or plastic wrap to seal it.

The butter can be stored for up to 3 weeks in the fridge or a couple of months in the freezer.

There is a plethora of combinations for tasty compound butters. I love a sweet compound butter when it comes to morning treats like oat scones—I make one with roasted spring strawberries, and another with a touch of crystallized ginger and toasted coconut. This lemony herb butter is a particularly handy stick to have in the fridge, ready to swipe on a crusty baguette, finish a quick sauté, or stir in a warm bowl of grains for a quick side dish.

While you could use a food processor to make this, I find the results are best when the mixing is done by hand, so you get a beautiful log of butter flecked with green and yellow bits rather than a murky green stick. When experimenting with your own combinations, using roasted or fried fruit or savory ingredients can help you add intense flavors to the butter while avoiding adding a lot of extra water and changing its structure too much.

preserved lemons

6 to 7 Meyer lemons, or more as
   needed

¹/₄ cup sea salt

1 tablespoon peppercorns

1 dried bay leaf

Thoroughly wash a wide-mouth pint-size mason jar with hot, soapy water. If using store-bought lemons, scrub them clean of any wax or residue. Cut the largest lemon in half and remove the seeds. This is the one you'll be using for juice.

Cut off the ends of the remaining lemons and slice into quarters.

Spoon about 2 tablespoons of the salt onto the bottom of the jar. Rub about 1 teaspoon of salt into four of the lemon quarters and pack to the bottom with a muddler or the handle of a wooden spoon. Don't be gentle; you want some of the juice to be released. Squeeze a bit of lemon juice on top. Repeat this process with the remaining lemons, using your fingers to rub 1 teaspoon of the salt into the flesh of four lemon slices, pressing them into the jar, and squeezing a bit of lemon juice on top each time.

When you get close to the top of the jar, push everything down a bit, being sure the lemons don't go over the shoulder of the jar. Sprinkle in the peppercorns and bay leaf. Squeeze in a bit more lemon juice and close the jar. Over the next few days, enough lemon juice should be produced to completely cover all the lemons. If not, add a bit more.

Allow the jar to sit at room temperature for a couple days, then store it in the fridge, shaking the jar every few days to move things around. Let them age for at least 1 month and preferably 3 months. They will keep for up to a year in the fridge.

To use them, scrape away and discard the salty flesh and slice the rind very thinly before adding it to your dish.

In this cookbook I use these lemons in the Moroccan Stuffed Squash (page 103), but once you have a jar of these available, you can play around with their tart personality in a number of dishes. They have a subtle pickled flavor as well as the tartness of lemon, which makes them a great addition to grain salads. You can also blend them into a dressing, serve them with chicken dishes, or use as a topping for fish such as salmon or trout. They really require only about 5 minutes of hands-on time, and the rest is just waiting, with a shake of the jar here and there.

pot of beans

MAKES 5 CUPS <

1 pound dried beans, such as cranberry, chickpeas, or great northern

2 dried bay leaves

1 teaspoon sea salt

Pick through the beans and remove any misshapen pieces. Rinse the beans in a colander, then put them in a big bowl and cover generously with cold water. Leave to soak for at least 6 hours or overnight.

Drain the beans and put them in a big pot with the bay leaves. Cover with fresh water by 2 inches. Bring to a gentle boil and cook, uncovered, until the beans are tender all the way through but not falling apart, 50 minutes to 1¹/₂ hours, depending on the type of bean. Add more water to the pot as needed if the pot is dry.

In the last few minutes of cooking, stir in the salt. Drain them of any excess water before using as needed.

Though I am not opposed to using canned beans in a pinch, I find that beans made from scratch are denser and have more character—almost "meaty"—with a bit of complexity to their structure. It is also less expensive to cook them from scratch, and doing so allows you to control the amount of salt. I salt my beans pretty liberally, but I'm still coming in with less sodium than a canned version.

If you don't need all 5 cups of the cooked beans that this recipe yields, fully cooked beans freeze well in plastic bags. Then when you need some for a soup or side, all you need to do is thaw.

grain cooking chart

The following chart includes the whole grains I use most often. I've included both quick- and slow-cooking grains, as you'll notice by the cooking times. Most of the quick-cooking ones, like couscous, millet, and quinoa, benefit from a good steaming off the heat with the lid on, which helps the grain retain moisture and end up light and fluffy.

Keep in mind that all these cooking times can vary a bit, depending on the freshness of the grains. Also, your preference for doneness may be different than mine. I tend to like my grains on the underdone side, so I make sure all the liquid has been absorbed and I fluff them with a fork to let out any pockets of steam.

The following directions are all for cooking 1 cup of the grain listed. As a general rule, bring the liquid to a simmer, add the grain, cover, and cook for the amount of time directed. If you won't use all the cooked grain within a week, you can freeze it in a plastic bag for up to three months.

GRAIN	RINSE?	WATER	TIME	YIELD	NOTES
Barley, pearled	Yes	2 1/2 cups	40 minutes	3 1/2 cups	Benefits from an hour soaking time before cooking.
Brown Rice	Yes	1 3/4 cups	45 minutes	2 cups	Bring rice to a simmer. Cover and cook without opening lid.
Cornmeal/ Polenta	No	3 1/2 cups	30 minutes	4 cups	Needs frequent stirring. Replace water with milk for creamy consistency.
Couscous	No	1 1/4 cups	10 minutes steam	2 1/2 cups	Add grain to simmering water. Turn off heat and cover to steam.
Farro	Yes	3 cups	40 minutes	3 cups	Benefits from an hour soaking time before cooking.
Millet	Yes	1 2/3 cups	20 minutes/ 5 minutes steam	3 cups	Bring to a simmer, cover, and cook, then steam off heat for 5 minutes.
Quinoa	Yes	1 2/3 cups	15 minutes/ 5 minutes steam	3 cups	Bring to a simmer, cover, and cook, then steam off heat for 5 minutes.
Soft Wheat Berries	Yes	1 3/4 cups	50 minutes	3 cups	Keep adding water for softer texture. Drain any excess water if necessary.
Steel-Cut Oats	No	3 cups	25 minutes	3 1/2 cups	Cooking time will vary based on desired texture. Add milk and cook uncovered another 5 minutes for creamy texture.
Wild Rice	Yes	2 3/4 cups	50 minutes	3 cups	Benefits from an hour soaking time before cooking.

with gratitude

We often find ourselves in places we wouldn't have expected, and this project was God's way of reminding me that the world is my oyster. Fear and caution seep from my pores, and I'm certain that this was the Lord's way of working in me—coaxing me to take a chance, to use my talent, and hopefully to serve people through it.

As I mentioned in the dedication, my husband, Hugh, made this book possible. The man has more confidence in me than I do, believes in my skill enough to nurture Sprouted Kitchen alongside me, and never ceases to impress me. Thank you for being my most critical taste tester and, more importantly, for taking the responsibility of documenting this project as seriously as you did. You are wonderful.

I am especially grateful to my recipe testers, Mollie Erickson, Ashley Walker, Dana Wooton, Ashley Rodriguez, Susan Turner, Monika Caruso, Maggie Rhyne, and Nicole Gulotta. I sent you recipes that often were a bit haphazard, and your feedback was invaluable. Thank you for your time, for your honest opinions, for your trips to the market, and for gently telling me that some directions actually made no sense at all. I was also so flattered that a number of longtime girlfriends wanted to help out too, just to give me another set of eyes. Thank you Courtney, Kristine, Shannon, Jessica, Nellie, and Jaclyn for being cheerleaders and testers for this project, as well as remarkable friends.

Mom, Dad, and Cydney—you guys may not be the recipe-testing type exactly, but you are a consistent support system. The newspaper and magazine clippings you shared with me from every food section you came across touched me. Whether it brought the inspiration you intended or not, your participation and encouragement meant a lot. My sister and I have been able to carve our own career paths in large part because of the selflessness of both of my parents. It has not gone unnoticed. Thank you for taking great care of your girls and supporting our creativity.

To Lisa Westmoreland, my editor at Ten Speed Press, thank you for believing in this project from the root of it and for being patient with my many questions and frantic emails. You walked me through writing a book, something I knew nothing about, and I am very grateful.

Toni Tajima—what a gracious personality you have. I knew from our first phone call that I liked you, and have never swayed from my first impression. From a creative stand-point, this whole process is intimidating, and the way you are so positively constructive and encouraging is impressive. Thank you for your time, talents, and kind disposition.

I am indebted to publicist Kristin Casemore for having the skills to share this book with more people than I expected.

Thanks to James Moes, the generous photographer mastermind, who took a few of the contributing photos of us in this book. To have the man who documented our wedding also capture a few photos of us "sprouted kitchening" was quite a treat. I feel terribly awkward in front of every camera besides yours. Thank you so much for your incredible skill.

Finally, a giant hug to every person who follows the Sprouted Kitchen blog. I never expected that the site would introduce me to the encouraging and truly kind people that it has. I love the feedback, questions, stories, and community that have blossomed there. Honestly. Thank you.

about us

SARA FORTE discovered a love for whole foods when she volunteered at an organic farm while working toward her English degree at Cal Poly, San Luis Obispo. The interest led to an internship in Italy at a bed-and-breakfast and cooking school, jobs at a few different markets, and eventually a food blog, Sprouted Kitchen (sproutedkitchen.com), that she produces with her husband, Hugh. She writes recipes and stories about life while he documents their whole food approach to eating well. Her work has been featured in *InStyle*, *Better Homes & Gardens*, *Sunset*, *Fine Cooking*, *Food & Wine*, *Whole Living*, *Every Day with Rachel Ray*, The Kitchn, Etsy, Food 52, and EcoSalon. The Sprouted Kitchen was a recent finalist in *Saveur*'s Best Food Blog Awards for Best Cooking and Best Food Photography. Sara continues to freelance in recipe development and take on small catering jobs on the side. They currently live in Dana Point, California, working, eating, and inspiring people to cook fresh, real food.

HUGH FORTE is a self-taught photographer whose work was born from traveling and wanting to document the life playing out around him. Although Hugh focuses most of his energy on wedding and lifestyle photography, he created Sprouted Kitchen as a gift to Sara so that they would have a creative outlet together, and he has since begun to experiment with a fresh approach to the art of food photography. With an aesthetic inspired largely by the natural beauty of the subject, his eye pairs well with Sara's cooking style. Hugh's work has been recognized by *Smithsonian*, *Photo District News*, and *Condé Nast Traveler*. While photography is both his profession and his passion, Hugh's time is also invested in great books, fun waves, and the pursuit of a really good cup of coffee.

index

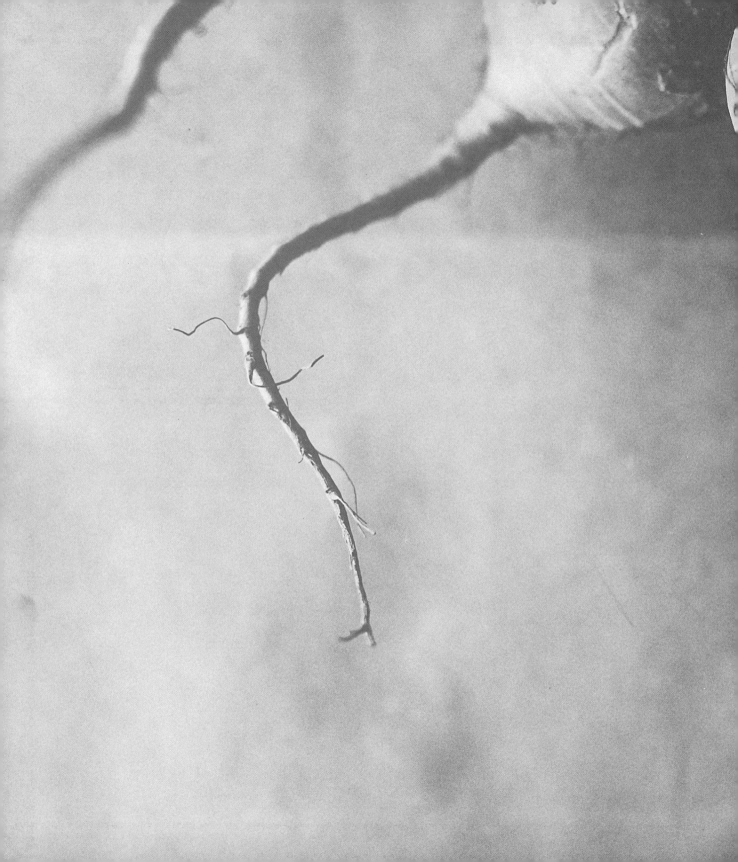